Rational Choice and Security Studies:
Stephen Walt and His Critics

International Security Readers

Strategy and Nuclear Deterrence (1984)

Military Strategy and the Origins of the First World War (1985)

Conventional Forces and American Defense Policy (1986)

The Star Wars Controversy (1986)

Naval Strategy and National Security (1988)

Military Strategy and the Origins of the First World War,
revised and expanded edition (1991)

—published by Princeton University Press

Soviet Military Policy (1989)

Conventional Forces and American Defense Policy, revised edition (1989)

Nuclear Diplomacy and Crisis Management (1990)

The Cold War and After: Prospects for Peace (1991)

America's Strategy in a Changing World (1992)

The Cold War and After: Prospects for Peace, expanded edition (1993)

Global Dangers: Changing Dimensions of International Security (1995)

The Perils of Anarchy: Contemporary Realism and International Security (1995)

Debating the Democratic Peace (1996)

East Asian Security (1996)

Nationalism and Ethnic Conflict (1997)

America's Strategic Choices (1997)

Theories of War and Peace (1998)

America's Strategic Choices, revised edition (2000)

Rational Choice and Security Studies: Stephen Walt and His Critics (2000)

The Rise of China (2000)

—published by The MIT Press

Rational Choice and Security Studies

Stephen Walt and His Critics

AN *International* *Security* READER

EDITED BY
Michael E. Brown
Owen R. Coté, Jr.
Sean M. Lynn-Jones
and Steven E. Miller

THE MIT PRESS
CAMBRIDGE, MASSACHUSETTS
LONDON, ENGLAND

Library of Congress Cataloging-in-Publication Data

Rational choice and security studies: Stephen Walt and his critics / edited by Michael E. Brown . . . [et al.].
    p. cm. — (International security readers)
  Articles in this reader were previously published in International Security, a quarterly journal.
  Includes bibliographical references.
  ISBN 0-262-52276-6 (pbk.: alk. paper)
  1. Security, International—Research. 2. Rational choice theory. 3. Walt, Stephen M.,
1955—Views on international security. I. Brown, Michael E. (Michael Edward), 1954– .
II. International security. III. Series.

JZ5588.R38 2000
327.1'01—dc21   00-023283

Contents

The Contributors

MICHAEL E. BROWN teaches in and is Director of Research for the National Security Studies Program, Edmund A. Walsh School of Foreign Service, Georgetown University, and is Editor of *International Security*.

OWEN R. COTÉ, JR. is Associate Director of the Security Studies Program at the Massachusetts Institute of Technology and Editor of *International Security*.

SEAN M. LYNN-JONES is Editor of *International Security* and a Research Associate at the Belfer Center for Science and International Affairs (BCSIA), John F. Kennedy School of Government, Harvard University.

STEVEN E. MILLER is the Editor-in-Chief of *International Security* and Director of the International Security Program at BCSIA.

BRUCE BUENO DE MESQUITA is a Senior Fellow at the Hoover Institution, Stanford University.

LISA L. MARTIN is Professor of Government at Harvard University.

JAMES D. MORROW is Senior Research Fellow at the Hoover Institution, Stanford University.

EMERSON M.S. NIOU is Associate Professor of Political Science at Duke University.

PETER C. ORDESHOOK is Professor of Political Science at the California Institute of Technology.

ROBERT POWELL is Robson Professor of Political Science at the University of California, Berkeley.

STEPHEN M. WALT is the Evron M. and Jeane J. Kirkpatrick Professor of International Affairs at the John F. Kennedy School of Government, Harvard University.

FRANK C. ZAGARE is Professor and Chair of the Department of Political Science at the University of Buffalo, State University of New York.

Acknowledgments

The editors gratefully acknowledge the assistance that has made this book possible. A deep debt is owed to all those as the Belfer Center for Science and International Affairs (BCSIA), Harvard University, who have played an editorial role at *International Security*. We are grateful for support from the Carnegie Corporation of New York. Special thanks go to Diane McCree and Meara Keegan Zaheer at BCSIA for their invaluable help in preparing this volume for publication.

Preface | *Sean M. Lynn-Jones*

This volume consists of a debate about the role of rational choice approaches—particularly formal, mathematical models—in the field of international security studies. It gathers together articles that were originally published in *International Security* in 1999. Stephen Walt opened the debate with "Rigor or Rigor Mortis? Rational Choice and Security Studies" in the journal's Spring 1999 issue. Walt's article presented a wide-ranging critique of the use of formal models and rational choice methods in security studies. At the invitation of the journal's editors, Bruce Bueno de Mesquita and James Morrow, Lisa Martin, Emerson Niou and Peter Ordeshook, Robert Powell, and Frank Zagare replied to Walt in the Fall 1999 issue. Walt replied to his critics in the same issue. We have assembled these articles into a short book in hopes of making this debate more readily available to a wider audience.

The debate presented in this volume is one manifestation of a broader controversy that has raged in political science and other social sciences in recent decades.[1] An increasing number of scholars has employed rational choice methods, including game theory and sophisticated formal mathematical models, in economics, sociology, political science, and other disciplines. These scholars generally assume that actors (whether voters, legislators, leaders, or nation-states) have a set of goals that they attempt to achieve through rational action. These assumptions can be used to build a logical set of propositions that predict how the actors will behave in various circumstances. In political science, formal models have been most prominent in the field of American politics, but game theory—long applied to the study of deterrence, crisis bargaining, and international cooperation—and formal models more generally have become more prominent in international security studies in recent years. Scholars who use formal models generally argue that their approach to the study of politics is more scientific and more likely to yield cumulative progress than other methods, such as case studies of historical episodes, analyses of ideas, norms, and beliefs, and applications of insights from psychology.

As rational choice approaches and formal models have become more prominent, scholars who prefer to use other methods have criticized both the approach and the scholars who use it. Critics of rational choice argue that formal models do not capture the complex realities of political action. However logical

---

1. For a brief overview of the controversial rise of rational choice and formal models in political science, see Jonathan Cohn, "Irrational Exuberance," *The New Republic*, October 25, 1999, pp. 25–31.

and precise, sets of equations cannot substitute for a deep understanding of, for example, a country's history and culture. Other critics point out that formal rational choice models often rest on unrealistic assumptions about actors' motives. In their view, formal methods contribute little to the understanding and solution of real-world political problems. Further criticisms have been leveled against the scholars who adhere to the rational choice approach. Many see "choicers" as intolerant of rival approaches and determined to assert hegemony over individual departments and the discipline of political science as a whole.[2]

In "Rigor or Rigor Mortis? Rational Choice and Security Studies," Stephen M. Walt argues that recent applications of formal rational choice theory have generated few new hypotheses or insights about contemporary security issues. He finds that the latest wave of technically complex, and mathematical formal theorizing has not significantly advanced our understanding of international security. Walt notes that the debate over the merits of rational choice approaches has important implications not only for the careers of individual scholars, but for the future of political science as a discipline. If rational choice theorists are dominant, they will inevitably privilege some questions, approaches, and methods over others.

According to Walt, formal rational choice approaches have the following five characteristics. First, rational choice theory assumes that social and political outcomes are the product of choices by individual, unitary actors. Second, the theory assumes that each actor seeks to maximize subjective expected utility. Third, we must be able to rank order the preferences of each actor, and the preferences must be transitive (if the actor prefers A to B, and B to C, then it prefers A to C). Fourth, formal theory entails specifying the structure of the game—identifying the set of players, their preferences, their information, and how they believe their moves are connected to possible outcome. Fifth, rational choice theorists attempt to identify the equilibria in games—choices of strategies that create situations from which no actor has an incentive to deviate unilaterally. Although some formal rational choice theorists might not agree with all of this characterization, Walt contends it aptly describes most recent formal work in security studies and international relations.

How should we evaluate recent formal rational choice scholarship in international security studies? Walt argues that three criteria should be used to

---

2. See the suggestions for further reading at the back of this book for a representative list of criticisms and defenses of rational choice.

judge rational choice theories—and all social science theories: (1) logical consistency and precision; (2) originality; and (3) empirical validity. Of these three, the latter two are especially important, because logical, consistent, and precise theories may still be trivial or false. Walt places special emphasis on the need to develop theories that "produce accurate and relevant knowledge about the human condition." He then assesses how rational choice models satisfy these three criteria.

Walt argues that rational choice methods can help to make theories more logically consistent and precise, but this does not necessarily make them superior to other approaches. Stating theories in formal, mathematical terms can be valuable. It makes assumptions apparent and enables scholars to determine whether predicted consequences follow from the initial premises. Nevertheless, Walt points out, nonformal theories also can be precise and logically consistent. Moreover, theories can contribute to knowledge even if they lack these two characteristics. Important theories in international relations, such as Kenneth Waltz's neorealist theory, have inconsistencies but they have been influential and have stimulated much creative scholarship. Walt suggests that logically consistent and precise formal theories may still be flawed if they are built on unrealistic assumptions or have multiple equilibria and thus fail to make clear predictions. The consistency and precision of formal theories also has a price. Complex formal mathematized theories are also less accessible to scholars and others not trained in formal methods and therefore are more difficult to evaluate critically and to apply practically.

Walt argues that recent formal rational choice scholarship in security studies often has failed to satisfy the second criterion for evaluating theories: it has not been creative or original. Recent formal work in security studies has not generated many new theories or hypotheses. Citing numerous examples of recent rational choice scholarship to support his arguments, Walt contends that this body of scholarship has exhibited a lack of originality in two ways. First, rational choice approaches have displayed "methodological overkill." Elaborate models have yielded trivial theoretical results. For example, formal models have shown that states do not initiate crises when the other side has military superiority, that states that will benefit from war are more likely to start wars, and that states form alliances to enhance their security. All of these findings are hardly surprising to scholars who do not use formal models. Second, formal models often produce "old wine in new bottles" by offering familiar arguments in a slightly new guise. Claims that "commitment problems" and "private information" cause wars that rational states would otherwise avoid, for example, reiterate long-standing arguments about the pernicious effects of anarchy and secrecy in international politics.

Walt acknowledges that formal approaches have yielded some new insights, including propositions about deterrence, arms races, alliances, and cooperation. But nonformal approaches have been at least as fruitful in generating new hypotheses and theories. Formal models actually may discourage creativity and originality by confining analyses to mathematically tractable two-party interactions and discouraging investigation of concrete empirical puzzles. Walt notes that deterrence theory traces its roots not to formal models, but to historical analysis and attempts to resolve U.S. policy dilemmas in the 1950s.

Turning to the third criterion for evaluating theories—empirical validity—Walt argues that most formal work in security studies fails to conduct any empirical tests and therefore lacks empirical support for its theoretical conclusions. In many cases, formal analyses rely on anecdotes or mathematical simulations. Some recent formal works have, however, offered extensive theoretical testing. Walt assesses two prominent examples: Bruce Bueno de Mesquita and David Lalman, *War and Reason: Domestic and International Imperatives;* and Emerson M.S. Niou, Peter C. Ordeshook, and Gregory F. Rose, *The Balance of Power: Stability in International Systems.*

Walt finds that the statistical analyses and case studies in *War and Reason* are not rigorous tests. Bueno de Mesquita and Lalman rely on crude indicators for concepts like "risk propensity," "utility," and "uncertainty." They do not offer precise measures for key variables. Their procedure of collapsing eight possible outcomes into a 2 X 2 table of observed and predicted outcomes lumps together cases in which the predicted outcome occurred and those in which it did not, thereby exaggerating the predictive performance of their model. The case studies in *War and Reason* do not provide more convincing evidence of the model's predictive capabilities. Walt contends that the evidence Bueno de Mesquita and Lalman offer from, for example, the Fashoda crisis, the Greco-Turkish confrontation over Cyprus, and the Sino-Indian War often contradicts the predictions of their model.

The Balance of Power, according to Walt, also fails to present empirical support for its theoretical predictions, despite its many virtues, which include clear presentation, candor about the limits of the model, and some counterintuitive predictions. Niou, Ordeshook, and Rose rely on ad hoc factors (e.g., the claim that the dispute over Alsace-Lorraine made a Franco-German alliance impossible between 1871 and 1914) to explain away alliance decisions that are inconsistent with their model. In addition, they do not show that states in the real world actually make decisions for the reasons identified by the model. For example, the model predicts that states will voluntarily transfer resources to another state to make an international system more stable, but actual states rarely transfer resources voluntarily. Finally, Walt argues that *The Balance of Power* unconvincingly claims that World War I began because Russia launched a preventive war against Germany—an interpretation that may support the model but flies in the face of most of the historical evidence.

Walt concludes that formal rational choice approaches to security studies are not inherently more valuable or scientific than other approaches. Formal methods may increase theoretical precision and consistency, but they have not offered powerful or creative new theories. Most recent formal work also has not been tested empirically. When scholars have offered empirical tests of formal theories, the evidence often has contradicted a model's predictions.

Walt also suggests that the rise of formal approaches imperils the ability of security studies to address actual security problems. Because rational choice methods have "relatively little to say about important real-world security issues" their increasing prominence may contribute to a "cult of irrelevance" in security studies. Formal theorists know a lot about highly technical methods of analysis, but little about politics and history. A field dominated by formal methods would be one divorced from contemporary security issues.

Walt argues that security studies should continue to embrace methodological pluralism. Formal rational choice theory should not be allowed to dominate the field. Instead, scholars should continue to pursue a diverse set of methods, including formal theory, statistical analysis, historical case studies, and constructivist analysis. If the field of security studies retains its intellectual and methodological diversity, it will continue to address important real-word security problems.

The next five essays in this volume offer replies to Walt's critique of formal rational choice theories and methods. In "Sorting Through the Wealth of Notions" Bruce Bueno de Mesquita and James Morrow defend formal rational choice approaches against Walt's criticisms. They argue that logical consistency is the most important criterion for evaluating theories. When theories are not logically consistent, virtually any hypothesis can be deduced from the theory, making empirical testing impossible. Logically inconsistent theories also do not offer useful policy prescriptions, because they can be used to justify different policy recommendations. Formal models force scholars to confront and eliminate logical inconsistencies in their theories by (1) requiring that assumptions be made explicit; (2) eliminating apparent contradictions by identifying the conditions for different conclusions; (3) integrating empirical regularities into a unified logical framework; and (4) identifying previously accepted results that do not follow from the theory. Bueno de Mesquita and Morrow offer examples of how articles that use formal models have achieved these four goals.

Bueno de Mesquita and Morrow also argue that formal models have generated many original insights and novel conclusions. They reconsider articles cited by Walt, pointing out that many of them offer new conclusions that Walt does not mention. Even when formal models reiterate conclusions reached through nonformal analysis they provide a logical basis for accepting some insights while rejecting others. In particular, they argue that the Bueno de Mesquita and Lalman, *War and Reason,* contains novel propositions and numerous empirical tests that have been replicated by other scholars.

Agreeing with Walt's view that social science should inform public policy, Bueno de Mesquita and Morrow argue that formal models can contribute to policy-relevant knowledge. They point to Bueno de Mesquita's "expected utility" model as an example of how basic research can generate a practical tool that offers policy advice. The Central Intelligence Agency and other U.S. government agencies have used this model.

In the subsequent essay, "The Contributions of Rational Choice: A Defense of Pluralism," Lisa Martin argues that as a consumer—not a producer—of formal theory she believes "the field of security studies would be severely impoverished if formal work were discouraged." Although Walt calls for diversity, Martin points out that his article is largely devoted to implicit calls for limiting the use of formal models in security studies. Martin offers three arguments in response to Walt. First, she contends that Walt overlooks how formal approaches have the great virtue of being able to generate integrated and logically coherent sets of propositions. In her view, Walt ignores this strength of formal models when he focuses on the originality—or lack thereof—of specific hypotheses derived from formal work. Building social-science theories entails creating complexes of related propositions, and formal modeling enables scholars to combine assumptions and hypotheses in a logical and coherent way.

Second, Martin argues that formalizing the insights of informal rational choice scholarship has important benefits. In response to what she calls the "Didn't Schelling already say that?" question, she answers that turning informal insights—even brilliant ones—into formal models often makes them more specific and enables scholars to identify the conditions under which they are true. Such formalization also contributes to logical consistency and coherence.

Third, Martin examines the contents of leading journals of international security studies in recent years to determine if formal work now dominates their pages. She finds that formal approaches are not overrepresented in security studies; only 13.1 percent of the 1994–98 articles that Martin surveys used formal models. Thus she concludes that formal models are hardly dominating the field and that formal work should be encouraged.

In "Return of the Luddites" Emerson Niou and Peter Ordeshook begin by agreeing that Walt is correct to note that much formal work in security studies ignores empirical reality and agree that some formal work is motivated by a desire for formalism for its own sake. After noting that Walt's critique is not aimed at rational choice approaches in general but at formalism in particular, they present five responses to Walt's arguments.

First, Niou and Ordeshook argue that Walt mistakenly places more value on theoretical originality and empirical validity than on logical consistency and precision. They contend that theories that are "incoherent, illogical, or imprecise" are difficult to evaluate and are unlikely to be empirically valid in any case—regardless of their originality. Formal models make it impossible to hide inconsistencies and flawed logic, even if they can be technically challenging to read and understand.

Second, Niou and Ordeshook take exception to Walt's claim that formal approaches have not generated creative or original theories. They point out that logical consistency in itself may be a creative theoretical contribution in a field where many leading theories are inconsistent and subject to numerous interpretations. Moreover, formal models represent theoretical progress when they contribute to specifying the conditions under which propositions derived informally are true. And the development of formal models is in itself a creative process.

Third, according to Niou and Ordeshook, Walt fails to show that alternatives to formal approaches have offered profound insights or systematic empirical testing. In other words, he does not present a "null hypothesis" against which to evaluate the contribution of formal scholarship.

Fourth, Niou and Ordeshook argue that Walt fails to understand how formal and empirical analyses are complementary. Many early informal applications of rational choice theories—including some that Walt praises—offer few, if any, empirical tests. Instead, scholars like Schelling, Olson, and Riker borrowed models and insights from formal theory and opened the way for further theorizing.

Finally, Niou and Ordeshook suggest that Walt misunderstands the process of scientific development. They contend that Walt mistakenly assumes that science consists of conducting controlled experiments that offer definitive tests of hypotheses. Most science does not conform to this image, however. In the natural sciences, scientific knowledge often advances through an ad hoc process of trying to solve real-world problems. Researchers are, however, held accountable for faulty judgments—something that rarely happens in political science, where the literature is replete with ambiguous theories and concepts, failed predictions, and poor policy advice.

Robert Powell, in "The Modeling Enterprise and Security Studies," defends the use of formal models on the grounds that this approach provides an "accounting standard" that makes it easier to communicate and assess arguments. Much of the nonformal literature in security studies contains ambiguous and contradictory statements and few robust empirical regularities. Powell offers three responses to Walt.

First, many of the most prominent arguments in contemporary security studies are neither transparent nor reproducible. Nonformal analyses often conceal their assumptions, making it impossible to tell what a theory predicts. Formal analyses can, for example, sharpen the distinction between concepts such as "the cost of fighting" and the "offense-defense balance." Mathematical language is often clearer and more concise than ordinary English language. Powell points out that recent formal work has shown that international anarchy does not induce concern for relative gains, and that the argument that states balance against power or threat is suspect, among other things. These contributions are a direct result of the transparency and reproducibility of formal models.

Second, Powell criticizes Walt for failing to appreciate how formal modeling has offered original insights. He argues that formal work on costly signals has introduced an important distinction between ex ante and ex post indicators, a distinction that was not present in earlier nonformal analyses such as Robert Jervis's *The Logic of Images in International Relations*. Powell also suggests that Walt conflates the generation of new ideas and deep insights with original theoretical contributions. Formal approaches have no monopoly on the former, but they often produce the latter.

Third, Powell responds to Walt's claim that recent formal work includes few empirical tests. He argues that some books and articles should not and need not include empirical tests if they are intended to elucidate new models or theories. This is also true of the nonformal literature, which includes important books and articles that offer few empirical tests. Kenneth Waltz's *Theory of International Politics* is a prominent example. Powell also points out that a considerable proportion of recent formal work in security studies does include empirical tests.

Powell concludes by noting that formal approaches have contributed to important post-Cold War debates on the democratic peace, ethnic conflict and international institutions. Formal models are not irrelevant to these important issues. He urges readers to read the recent literature so that they can judge the contribution of formal approaches for themselves.

Frank Zagare's "All Mortis, No Rigor" lauds Walt for recognizing that formal methods ensure logical consistency and enhance clarity, but faults him for abandoning these virtues in his article. He also argues that Walt is wrong to claim that formal models would be misleading if decisonmakers do not use the decisionmaking processes attributed to them by rational choice theory.

Zagare responds to Walt's critique of recent formal scholarship in security studies by defending his own work against Walt's charge that it exemplifies "methodological overkill." He argues that Walt examined only one of many articles that Zagare has co-authored with Marc Kilgour. Zagare claims that this body of work differs from classical deterrence theory, particularly in treating threat credibility as a variable, and reaches different conclusions.

Zagare also argues that formal models are valuable even when they do not advance novel propositions, because they give arguments logical structure and make it possible to assess how different assumptions lead to different conclusions.

Finally, Zagare replies to Walt's charge that formal theorists have not conducted systematic empirical tests of their theories. Noting that some critics say that Walt's own work lacks such tests, he argues that formal models can and should be empirically tested. The fact that some formal theorists have not offered empirical tests reflects the division of labor in political science, not the limitations of formal models.

In this volume's final essay, "A Model Disagreement," Walt replies to his critics. He groups his responses into five categories. First, Walt responds to critics who claim that he undervalues logical consistency and precision, which they regard as the sine qua non of any scientific theory. He argues that he believes that logical consistency is highly desirable, but reiterates that it is not the only criterion by which theories should be judged. In his view, logical consistency by itself does not make a theory good. Creative new theories are valuable even when they rest on unidentified assumptions or contain inconsistencies. These problems are easier to resolve when a theory offers an important argument, and wholly contradictory theories will not last long. Formalization is not the only way to make precise, logically consistent arguments. Moreover, most formal work does not attempt to identify and resolve inconsistencies in nonformal theories, but instead identifies assumptions and conditions under which hypotheses operate. Walt points out that his critics identify only one example of how formal analysis has corrected a logically contradictory argument.

Second, Walt replies to arguments that he overlooks the creativity of formal models. He points out that he did not claim that building models requires no creative insight, but instead argued that formal modeling rarely leads to "new, empirically valid insights about international security." Walt examines each of the examples of apparently creative formal work that Bueno de Mesquita and Morrow and Powell present. He argues that these articles offer few new theoretical claims and some do not even include formal models.

Third, Walt argues that his critics do not seriously challenge his claim that formal modelers have not offered rigorous tests of their conclusions. He notes that the article cited by Bueno de Mesquita as empirical support for *The War Trap* actually offers little support. Walt suggests that Niou and Ordeshook seem to abandon the idea of empirical testing entirely. Walt also points out that he believes several otherwise praiseworthy nonformal works in international security studies could have been better if they had included more empirical tests. In response to claims that there should be a division of labor in which formal theorists build models and leave the testing to others, he points out that formal modelers do not seem to place a high value on testing and that there would be few scholars to do any testing if security studies is dominated by formal modelers.

Fourth, Walt reiterates that nonformal analyses have generated more useful policy-relevant knowledge than formal models. Replying to Bueno de Mesquita's claim that his model has been used and praised by government agencies, Walt argues that Bueno de Mesquita's published forecasts have not been very accurate and that former senior CIA officials report that Bueno de Mesquita's model has not had an impact on U.S. policy.

Fifth, Walt replies to Martin's argument that formal modelers do not dominate leading journals in security studies. He argues that the real issue were not the proportion of articles that use formal models, but the hegemonic aspirations of the formal modelers. In his view, the replies to his article confirm that formal modelers are intolerant of other approaches and do not embrace the goal of intellectual diversity. Walt points out that several of his critics deride nonformal approaches and claim that formal models are the wave of the future in security studies and political science more generally.

Walt concludes that the field of security studies should retain a healthy intellectual diversity. The field will suffer if any one approach dominates.

The essays collected here do not offer a complete picture of the debate between formal rational choice theorists and their critics. Similar arguments exist in fields other than international security studies, and in disciplines other than political science. A sampling of the relevant literature that criticizes and defends formal models appears in the "Suggestions for Further Reading" at the end of this volume.

These essays also do not represent the last word in the debate between proponents and opponents of formal models. This controversy will continue to rage in political science and other disciplines. The outcome of this debate will have much influence on which scholars, approaches, and topics become most prominent in international security studies. We hope that this volume contributes to this important debate.

Rigor or Rigor Mortis? | *Stephen M. Walt*

Rational Choice and Security Studies

The past decade has witnessed a growing controversy over the status of formal approaches in political science, and especially the growing prominence of formal rational choice theory. Rational choice models have been an accepted part of the academic study of politics since the 1950s, but their popularity has grown significantly in recent years.[1] Elite academic departments are now expected to include game theorists and other formal modelers in order to be regarded as "up to date," graduate students increasingly view the use of formal rational choice models as a prerequisite for professional advancement, and research employing rational choice methods is becoming more widespread throughout the discipline.[2]

Is the increased prominence of formal rational choice theory necessary, inevitable, and desirable? Advocates of formal rational choice approaches assert that these techniques are inherently more scientific than other analytic

Stephen M. Walt is Professor of Political Science and Master of the Social Science Collegiate Division at the University of Chicago. He will join the faculty of the John F. Kennedy School of Government at Harvard University in July 1999.

I thank the following individuals for their comments on earlier drafts of this article: Graham Allison, Robert Art, Michael Desch, George Downs, Erik Gartzke, Charles Glaser, Joseph Grieco, Robert Jervis, John Mearsheimer, Barry Posen, Jack Snyder, Stephen Van Evera, and the participants at seminars at Princeton, Rutgers, Duke, and the John M. Olin Institute for Strategic Studies at Harvard. Barry O'Neill provided an exceptionally detailed and useful set of criticisms, for which I am especially grateful, and Ann Ducharme, David Edelstein, and Seth Jones were able research assistants and made valuable suggestions as well.

1. Seminal early applications of rational choice theory include Anthony Downs, *An Economic Theory of Democracy* (New York: Harper and Row, 1957); Gordon Tullock and James Buchanan, eds., *The Calculus of Consent* (Ann Arbor: University of Michigan Press, 1962); Thomas C. Schelling, *The Strategy of Conflict* (Cambridge, Mass.: Harvard University Press, 1960); and Mancur Olson, *The Logic of Collective Action: Public Goods and the Theory of Groups* (Cambridge, Mass.: Harvard University Press, 1965). Surveys of the basic literature include Dennis Mueller, ed., *Public Choice II* (Cambridge, U.K.: Cambridge University Press, 1989); James Alt and Kenneth Shepsle, eds., *Perspectives on Positive Political Economy* (Cambridge, U.K.: Cambridge University Press, 1990); and Peter C. Ordeshook, ed., *Models of Strategic Choice in Politics* (Ann Arbor: University of Michigan Press, 1989). An excellent introductory textbook is James D. Morrow, *Game Theory for Political Scientists* (Princeton, N.J.: Princeton University Press, 1995).
2. According to one estimate, rational choice scholarship now comprises nearly 40 percent of the published articles in the *American Political Science Review*, and another scholar reports that 22 percent of the *APSR* articles published between 1980 and 1993 were rational choice in orientation. Similarly, the annual report of the *APSR*'s editor suggests that 15–20 percent of all ASPR submissions and published articles were rational choice in orientation. See Donald Green and Ian Shapiro,

International Security, Vol. 23, No. 4 (Spring 1999), pp. 5–48
© 1999 by the President and Fellows of Harvard College and the Massachusetts Institute of Technology.

approaches, and argue that the use of more sophisticated models has produced major theoretical advances.[3] They are also prone to portray skeptics as methodological Luddites whose opposition rests largely on ignorance. Thus Robert Bates draws a distinction between "social scientists" and "area specialists" (a distinction that implies the latter are not scientific), and suggests that the discipline is finally "becoming equipped to handle area knowledge in rigorous ways." According to Bates, these "rigorous ways" are rational choice models, and he chastises area experts for raising "principled objection to innovations . . . while lacking the training fully to understand them."[4]

Not surprisingly, other scholars have greeted such claims with considerable skepticism, and argue that rational choice theory has yet to produce a substantial number of important new hypotheses or well-verified empirical predictions.[5] Indeed, some critics of rational choice methods question whether formal techniques are of any value whatsoever, and regard the modeling community as a group of narrow-minded imperialists seeking to impose its preferred method on the entire discipline.[6]

Pathologies of Rational Choice Theory: A Critique of Applications in Political Science (New Haven, Conn.: Yale University Press, 1995), p. 2; Norman Schofield, "Rational Choice and Political Economy," *Critical Review,* Vol. 9, Nos. 1–2 (Winter–Spring 1995), p. 210, n. 10–12; and Ada W. Finifter, "Report of the Editor of the *American Political Science Review, 1996–97,*" *PS: Political Science and Politics,* Vol. 30, No. 4 (December 1997), pp. 783–791.

3. For example, the late William Riker once argued that social science laws "must be encased in a deductive theory," and suggested that rational choice models were the basis for the only successful social science theories. Similarly, Bruce Bueno de Mesquita argues that "formal, explicit theorizing takes intellectual precedence over empiricism," and Peter Ordeshook once claimed that "understanding politics requires sophisticated tools of deduction. . . . If mathematics is a necessary part of that analysis, then such mathematics is necessarily a part of political theory." See Riker, "Political Science and Rational Choice," in Alt and Shepsle, *Perspectives on Positive Political Economy,* pp. 168, 175–177; Bueno de Mesquita, "Toward a Scientific Understanding of International Conflict: A Personal View," *International Studies Quarterly,* Vol. 29, No. 2 (June 1985), pp. 121–136; and Peter C. Ordeshook, "Introduction," in Ordeshook, *Models of Strategic Choice in Politics,* p. 2.

4. See Robert Bates, "Letter from the President: Area Studies and the Discipline," *APSA-CP: Newsletter of the APSA Organized Section on Comparative Politics,* Vol. 7, No. 1 (Winter 1996), pp. 1–2; Bates, "Area Studies and the Discipline: A Useful Controversy," *PS: Political Science and Politics,* Vol. 30, No. 2 (June 1997), pp. 166–169; and Bernard Grofman, "The Gentle Art of Rational Choice Bashing," in Grofman, ed., *Information, Participation, and Choice* (Ann Arbor: University of Michigan Press, 1993).

5. See Green and Shapiro, *Pathologies of Rational Choice Theory;* Raymond Wolfinger, "The Rational Citizen Faces Election Day, or What Rational Choice Theories Don't Tell You about American Elections," in M. Kent Jennings and Thomas E. Mann, eds., *Elections at Home and Abroad: Essays in Honor of Warren E. Miller* (Ann Arbor: University of Michigan Press, 1993); and Lars Udehn, *The Limits of Public Choice: A Sociological Critique of the Economic Theory of Politics* (New York: Routledge, 1996).

6. See, for example, Chalmers Johnson and E.B. Keehn, "A Disaster in the Making: Rational Choice and Asian Studies," *National Interest,* No. 36 (Summer 1994), pp. 14–22; and Johnson, "Preconcep-

The stakes in this dispute are considerable. Because technical proficiency is often used as a surrogate for professional competence—and even to define what constitutes "legitimate" scholarship in a particular field—the outcome of this debate will have a powerful impact on the basic nature of the social sciences and on the allocation of finite academic resources. To put it bluntly, if reliance on formal methods becomes the sine qua non of "scientific" inquiry, then scholars who do not use them will eventually be marginalized within their respective fields. Like most methodological debates, therefore, the struggle has been quite contentious.[7]

One unfortunate result of this polarization has been the stifling of genuine debate on these issues. Instead of debating and acknowledging the actual strengths and weaknesses of competing research traditions, scholars are increasingly reluctant to criticize one another openly for fear of being seen as intolerant. Because such a reputation can have chilling effects on one's professional prospects (particularly for younger scholars), the result is a narrowing of intellectual exchange. This is antithetical to scientific progress, which is furthered by an unfettered clash of ideas.[8]

What is at stake goes beyond the evolution of particular academic departments or the career prospects of individual scholars, however. Much more important, the outcome of this debate will also guide the nature of scholarly discourse on important political topics and shape the intellectual capital of the scholarly community. Subfields that are dominated by rational choice theorists will inevitably emphasize certain types of work over others, will privilege certain questions at the expense of others, and will prize certain analytical talents rather than others.[9] Thus the debate over the role of formal rational choice theory will have a powerful effect on what we think we know about

tion vs. Observation, or the Contributions of Rational Choice Theory and Area Studies to Contemporary Political Science," *PS: Political Science and Politics*, Vol. 30, No. 2 (June 1997), pp. 170–174.
7. Past examples include the *Methodonstreit* among economic theorists in Germany in the nineteenth century, the struggle between institutional and neoclassical economists before and after World War II, and the "great debate" between so-called behavioralists and traditionalists in American political science (including international relations) in the 1960s. See Klaus Knorr and James N. Rosenau, *Contending Approaches to International Politics* (Princeton, N.J.: Princeton University Press, 1967); and Yuval P. Yonay, *The Struggle over the Soul of Economics: Institutionalist and Neoclassical Economics in America between the Wars* (Princeton, N.J.: Princeton University Press, 1998).
8. An exception to this observation is the special issue of *Critical Review*, Vol. 9, Nos. 1–2 (Winter–Spring 1995), entitled "Rational Choice Theory and Politics."
9. The same is true for fields that employ nonformal approaches, of course. The central point is simply that the content of a field of inquiry is inevitably shaped by the techniques and procedures that are used to study it.

politics, and thus on what the academic community will be able to contribute to the wider public debate on important social issues.

This article seeks to advance this debate by evaluating the contribution of recent formal work in the field of security studies. Formal rational choice theory has been part of security studies for several decades, but recent formal scholarship is quite different from the seminal early work of scholars like Thomas Schelling, Daniel Ellsberg, or Mancur Olson. "First-wave" theorists like Schelling used simple formal illustrations and did not place much emphasis on mathematical rigor. Indeed, Schelling explicitly warned against the tendency for social scientists "to treat the subject of strategy as though it were, or should be, solely a branch of mathematics."[10] The "second wave" of formal theorizing has largely ignored Schelling's warning and placed far more emphasis on formal proofs and mathematical derivations. The question, therefore, is whether this latest wave of formal theorizing has contributed significantly to our understanding of international security.

My argument is straightforward. The central aim of social science is to develop knowledge that is relevant to understanding important social problems. Among other things, this task requires theories that are precise, logically consistent, original, and empirically valid. Formal techniques facilitate the construction of precise and deductively sound arguments, but recent efforts in security studies have generated comparatively few new hypotheses and have for the most part not been tested in a careful and systematic way. The growing technical complexity of recent formal work has not been matched by a corresponding increase in insight, and as a result, recent formal work has relatively little to say about contemporary security issues.

Two caveats should be noted before proceeding. First, this article does not offer a comprehensive analysis of recent formal work in security studies. Space does not permit me to discuss every application of formal theory to a security studies topic; instead, I have concentrated on the work of a number of prominent figures in the rational choice field and on scholarship that has been regarded by members of that subfield as especially sophisticated. By focusing on some of the best and most widely cited work, therefore, my sample is if anything biased in favor of formal approaches.

Second, this article does not compare the relative merits of formal theory with other methodological approaches. Such a comparison would be extremely valuable, but a proper assessment would require far more space than is avail-

---

10. Schelling, *Strategy of Conflict*, pp. 10–11, n. 4.

able here. Moreover, even if one were able to show that a particular approach had been especially productive, that would hardly mean that alternative research techniques should be entirely discarded.

The remainder of this article is organized as follows. The first section summarizes the basic principles of rational choice theory and describes the literature under scrutiny in the rest of the article. The second section describes the essential aims of social science and discusses several criteria for judging a body of scholarship. I argue that three criteria are especially important: precision and consistency, originality, and empirical validity. The third, fourth, and fifth sections apply these criteria to recent formal work in security studies, focusing on a number of especially important or prominent examples. The last section summarizes my assessment and offers some concluding remarks about the place of formal theory in this field.

What Is Formal Theory?

Formal rational choice theory is defined "more by the *method* of theory construction than by the *content* of its theories."[11] It refers to the use of mathematical models to derive propositions from a set of basic premises. The use of mathematics helps ensure logical consistency among the propositions, especially when dealing with complex relationships where the use of ordinary language might lead to logical errors or vague predictions.

Formal rational choice theory is more than just the assumption of purposive behavior on the part of social actors (as in the familiar "rational actor" assumption). Similarly, it does not refer to any scholarship that uses simple game theory concepts like the "prisoner's dilemma" or "mixed strategies" primarily for heuristic purposes or as an illustrative analogy. Strictly speaking, formal theory involves the construction of specific mathematical models intended to represent particular real-world situations and the use of mathematics to identify the specific solutions ("equilibria") for the model(s).[12]

---

11. See David Lalman, Joe Oppenheimer, and Piotr Swistak, "Formal Rational Choice Theory: A Cumulative Science of Politics," in Ada W. Finifter, ed., *Political Science: State of the Discipline II* (Washington, D.C.: American Political Science Association, 1993), p. 78 (emphasis in original).
12. Barry O'Neill makes a useful distinction between (1) "proto-game theory" (where formal ideas provide a convenient vocabulary or offer useful analogies), (2) "low game theory" (where solutions to specific games are used to analyze particular social interactions), and (3) "high game theory" (where scholars construct general proofs for whole classes of games). See O'Neill, "Game Theory and the Study of Deterrence in War," in Paul C. Stern, Robert Axelrod, Robert Jervis, and Roy Radner, eds., *Perspectives on Deterrence* (London: Oxford University Press, 1989), p. 135. Prominent

In security studies, formal rational choice theory usually means the use of game theory. Game theory is a set of techniques for analyzing individual decisions, in situations where each player's payoff depends in part on what the other players are expected to do. Game theory thus differs from decision-theoretic approaches, which analyze individual utility maximization against an exogenous, noncalculating environment. Because security studies generally focuses on situations where actors frequently try to anticipate what others will do, and where the outcome for each actor will be affected by the choices that others make, the attractiveness of game theory is not surprising.[13]

Formal rational choice theorists do not agree on everything, of course, and there are important epistemological and methodological differences within the modeling community. Nonetheless, most applications in the field of international relations or security studies employ the following basic assumptions and techniques.

1. Rational choice theory is *individualistic:* social and political outcomes are viewed as the collective product of *individual* choices (or as the product of choices made by unitary actors).

2. Rational choice theory assumes that each actor seeks to maximize its "subjective expected utility." Given a particular set of preferences and a fixed array of possible choices, actors will select the outcome that brings the greatest expected benefits.

3. The specification of actors' preferences is subject to certain constraints: (a) an actor's preferences must be complete (meaning we can rank order their preference for different outcomes); and (b) preferences must be transitive (if A is preferred to B and B to C, then A is preferred to C).[14]

4. Constructing a formal theory requires the analyst to specify the *structure* of the game. This typically means identifying the set of players, the likelihoods

---

examples of proto-game theory include Robert Jervis, "Cooperation under the Security Dilemma," *World Politics,* Vol. 30, No. 2 (January 1978), pp. 167–214; and Robert O. Keohane, *After Hegemony: Cooperation and Discord in the World Political Economy* (Princeton, N.J.: Princeton University Press, 1984). This article focuses primarily on low game theory, which accurately describes the bulk of recent formal work in security studies.

13. I have not examined the extensive use of operations research and other decision-theoretic techniques in the analysis of military policy, largely because this work has had less impact in the social sciences. An encyclopedic survey is Barry O'Neill, "Game Theory Models of War and Peace," in Robert Aumann and Sergiu Hart, eds., *Handbook of Game Theory with Economic Applications,* Volume 2 (Amsterdam: Elsevier Science, 1994).

14. A more demanding condition is that the actors' utility functions are consistent with the Von Neumann-Morgenstern expected utility theorem. This theorem imposes additional constraints (such as the exclusion of infinite utilities), but is not necessary in simple contexts. See Morrow, *Game Theory for Political Scientists,* chap. 2.

of each player's pattern of preferences, each player's information at every choice point, and how they see their moves as connected to the possible outcomes.

5. Once the game is fully specified, the analyst usually looks for its *equilibrium*. An equilibrium is an assignment of strategies to the players, such that each player's strategy maximizes his or her expected utility, given that the others use their assigned strategies. Thus an equilibrium is a strategy from which a rational actor would have no incentive to deviate unilaterally.[15]

Within a formal rational choice model, therefore, an equilibrium is a prediction. If the game structure is an accurate representation of the phenomenon in question, and if there are no mathematical mistakes, the equilibria of the game identify the only outcomes that are logically possible. These equilibria form the basis for any subsequent empirical testing.[16]

As noted above, there are important differences among formal theorists regarding the epistemological status of these models. For example, formal theorists are divided between those who endorse a "thin" conception of rationality (which assumes only that the actors choose rationally to achieve whatever goals they may have) and those who rely on stronger assumptions ("thick rationality") about each actor's preferences. In the latter case, the analyst assumes that preferences are consistently ordered and also specifies what those preferences are (e.g., that the actors seek to maximize power, or wealth, or whatever). There are also disputes over whether rational choice theories must merely be consistent with the observed outcome, or whether they must also be consistent with the actual process by which decisions are made.[17] This

---

15. More precisely, this is the definition of a "Nash equilibrium," first established by John Nash. See ibid., pp. 91–98. For a formal discussion, see David M. Kreps, "Nash Equilibrium," in John Eatwell, Murray Milgate, and Peter Newman, eds., *The New Palgrave: A Dictionary of Economics: Game Theory* (New York: W.W. Norton, 1989), pp. 167–177.

16. As William Riker puts it, "Equilibria are valuable, indeed essential in theory in social science because they are identified consequences of decisions that are necessary and sufficient to bring them about. An explanation is . . . the assurance that an outcome must be the way it is because of antecedent conditions. This is precisely what an equilibrium provides." See Riker, "Political Science and Rational Choice," p. 175.

17. The question is whether the actors must *consciously* select the course of action that will maximize their expected utility through a process of reasoning that is at least roughly consistent with the logic of the model. According to Jon Elster, a proper rational choice explanation requires that "the action must not only be rationalized by the desire and the belief, but it must also be caused by them and, moreover, caused 'in the right way.'" See his "Introduction," in Elster, ed., *Rational Choice* (New York: New York University Press, 1986), p. 16; and Terry Moe, "On the Scientific Status of Rational Choice Theory," *American Journal of Political Science*, Vol. 23, No. 1 (February 1979), pp. 215–243.

latter issue does not affect the construction of a formal model, but it is critical to any effort to test its implications.[18]

How to Judge Social Science Theories

The fundamental aim of social science is to develop *useful knowledge* about human social behavior. Such knowledge may take the form of a deeper and more accurate understanding of the past, or the elaboration of a new theory that explains some important aspect of human conduct, or a largely descriptive account of a particular social group or event. Whatever its precise form, the essence of the enterprise is the discovery of powerful, well-founded claims about human behavior. Social science should not be merely an intellectual exercise undertaken for the benefit of its practitioners. Given that what we know (or think we know) about human nature and social institutions can have powerful effects on the fates of whole societies, social science should always strive to produce accurate and relevant knowledge about the human condition.

Given this basic objective, there are three main criteria for evaluating social science theories.

First, a theory should be *logically consistent* and *precise*. Other things being equal, theories that are stated precisely and that are internally consistent are preferable to theories that are vague or partly contradictory. An inconsistent theory is problematic because (some of) the conclusions or predictions may not follow logically from the initial premises. In this sense, an inconsistent theory creates a false picture of the world. Inconsistent theories are also more difficult to test because it is harder to know if the available evidence supports the theory. Similar problems arise when a theory is vague, because a wider range of empirical outcomes will be consistent with the theory as stated. Precision also means identifying underlying assumptions and boundary conditions, which helps us guard against applying the theory in circumstances for which it is not suited.

The second criterion is *degree of originality*. Although the level of originality can be difficult to measure and subject to dispute, it is still one of the most prized features of any scientific theory. We prefer creative and original theories because they tell us things that we did not already know and help us see familiar phenomena in a new way. A novel theory imposes order upon phe-

---

18. A good summary of these issues is found in Green and Shapiro, *Pathologies of Rational Choice Theory.*

nomena that were previously hard to understand, and solves conceptual or empirical puzzles that earlier theories could not adequately explain. Not surprisingly, therefore, both natural and social scientists place a premium on the creation of new ideas.[19]

The (final) criterion is *empirical validity*. The justification for this criterion should be obvious as well: the only way to determine if a theory is truly useful is to compare its predictions against an appropriate body of evidence. Theories may be tested either by examining the correlation between independent and dependent variables (i.e., do they covary in the manner predicted by the theory?) or by testing the causal logic directly through detailed process-tracing.[20]

When evaluating a particular research tradition, therefore, we want to know if its propositions receive adequate empirical support. Are efforts to test key propositions carefully done, and are the results consistent with the theory? Other things being equal, a research tradition that ignores or discounts this requirement is being too easy on itself.

These criteria provide a set of hurdles that any social science approach must try to overcome. Although all three are important, the latter two criteria—originality and empirical validity—are especially prized. A consistent, precise yet trivial argument is of less value than a bold new conjecture that helps us understand some important real-world problem, even if certain ambiguities and tensions remain. Similarly, a logically consistent but empirically false theory is of little value, whereas a roughly accurate but somewhat imprecise theory may be extremely useful even though it is still subject to further refinement.[21] We do not expect every article or book to receive a high score on

---

19. Famous examples of especially original and fruitful theories include Darwin's theory of natural selection, Newton's mechanics, and Einstein's theory of relativity. In the social sciences, one might point to Keynesian economic theory, collective goods theory, deterrence theory, the theory of bureaucratic politics, and the application of cognitive and social psychology to international conflict. Although some of these theories later fell from favor, each was properly regarded as a creative and potentially valuable conceptual vision, and each spawned a large and influential literature.

20. On these methods of theory testing, see Stephen Van Evera, *Guide to Methods for Students of Political Science* (Ithaca, N.Y.: Cornell University Press, 1997).

21. Thus Christopher Achen and Duncan Snidal argue that the first wave of rational deterrence theory was "astonishingly fecund, both for theory and for policy," and of "immense practical importance." Yet the theory was not developed through formal modeling and contains many features that Achen and Snidal judge to be "woefully underconceptualized." See Achen and Snidal, "Rational Deterrence Theory and Comparative Case Studies," *World Politics*, Vol. 41, No. 2 (January 1989), pp. 153, 159.

all three criteria, of course, but we have reason to be skeptical if a particular research tradition consistently slights one or more of them.

Let us now consider how well recent formal work meets these standards.

Logical Consistency and Precision

This section examines whether formal rational choice methods contribute to the development of logical and precise theories. After describing the virtues of formalization, I explain why formalization is neither necessary nor sufficient for scientific progress and consider some of the costs that it imposes. I conclude that although rational choice models can help increase the precision of our theories, this contribution does not justify privileging them over other social science approaches.

WHY USE FORMAL MODELS?

In social science, the main virtue of formalization is its contribution to logical consistency and precision. According to James Morrow, the primary advantage of formal modeling is "the *rigor and precision of argument* that it requires."[22] Not surprisingly, therefore, scholars who use these methods place a very high value on this criterion. Thus Bruce Bueno de Mesquita has declared that "logical consistency is a fundamental requirement of all [scientific] hypotheses," and he further suggests that "our main problem [in the study of international conflict] is not a lack of facts . . . but a lack of rigorously derived hypotheses that can render our facts informative."[23] Properly employed, the formal language of mathematics can impart greater precision to an argument, and helps guard against inconsistencies arising either from a failure to spell out the causal logic in detail or from the ambiguities of normal language.[24]

---

22. See Morrow, *Game Theory for Political Scientists*, p. 6 (emphasis added).
23. Bueno de Mesquita, "Toward a Scientific Understanding of International Conflict," p. 128. See also Steven Brams and D. Marc Kilgour, *Game Theory and National Security* (New York: Basil Blackwell, 1988), p. 2. The mathematical economist Gerard Debreu offers a similar defense of abstract modeling, arguing that "economic theory has had to adhere to the rules of logical discourse and must renounce the facility of internal inconsistency. A deductive structure that tolerates a contradiction does so under the penalty of being useless, since any statement can be derived flawlessly and immediately from that contradiction." See Debreu, "The Mathematization of Economic Theory," *American Economic Review*, Vol. 81, No. 1 (March 1991), pp. 2–3. For a typically witty rebuttal of Debreu's claims, see Deidre N. McCloskey, *The Vices of Economists—The Virtues of the Bourgeoisie* (Amsterdam: Amsterdam University Press, 1996), pp. 78–81.
24. Kenneth Arrow offered a similar assessment more than four decades ago, writing that "mathematics . . . is distinguished from the other languages habitually used by the social scientists chiefly by its superior clarity and consistency." Arrow, "Mathematical Models in the Social Sciences," in Daniel Lerner and Harold D. Lasswell, eds., *The Policy Sciences* (Stanford, Calif.: Stanford University

In this sense, expressing an existing theory in formal language provides one type of test: Do the predicted consequences follow logically from the stated premises? In this sense, formalization can give us greater confidence in theories that were originally stated in verbal form. Formalization can also make the assumptions that drive a conclusion more apparent, thereby spurring further investigation and discouraging any tendency to overgeneralize.

These virtues should not be dismissed lightly. In the field of security studies, for example, formal analysis has shown that certain widely accepted propositions were not strictly deducible from the standard premises, as in Robert Powell's formal demonstration that the state with higher resolve may not always prevail in a nuclear crisis.[25] Similarly, a formal model can suggest new ways to interpret a body of empirical data, as in James Fearon's use of a simple bargaining model to show how selection effects can alter how one interprets historical cases of extended deterrence.[26] Finally, formal theory can also provide the tools to analyze especially complex interactions, where one might not be able to work through the causal processes in purely verbal form. Thus, even if formal techniques made no other contribution, their capacity to verify and maintain logical consistency is an undeniable asset.

WHY FORMALIZATION IS NEITHER NECESSARY NOR SUFFICIENT FOR SCIENTIFIC PROGRESS

This endorsement of formalization needs to be qualified in several important respects, however. First, the use of formal techniques is not a prerequisite for logical consistency. Many nonformal works of natural and social science contain precise, logically consistent theories, which casts doubt on the claim that formal methods are a necessary part of science.[27] Darwin's theory of natural

---

Press, 1951), p. 129. See also David M. Kreps, *Game Theory and Economic Modelling* (Oxford, U.K.: Oxford University Press, 1990), pp. 6–7.

25. See Robert Powell, *Nuclear Deterrence Theory: The Search for Credibility* (Cambridge, U.K.: Cambridge University Press, 1990).

26. James D. Fearon, "Signaling versus the Balance of Power and Interests: An Empirical Test of a Crisis Bargaining Model," *Journal of Conflict Resolution*, Vol. 38, No. 2 (June 1994), pp. 236–269. Strictly speaking, one does not need a formal model to recognize that selection effects should be taken into account when interpreting the success or failure of deterrence. For a nonformal discussion of the same point, see Jack Levy, "Quantitative Studies of Deterrence Success and Failure," in Stern et al., *Perspectives on Deterrence*, pp. 117–120.

27. Examples from the social sciences include Benjamin Cohen's restatements of the various strands of Marxist theory in Cohen, *The Question of Imperialism: The Political Economy of Dominance and Dependence* (New York: Basic Books, 1973); Andrew J.R. Mack, "Why Big Nations Lose Small Wars: The Politics of Asymmetric Conflict," *World Politics*, Vol. 27, No. 2 (January 1975), pp. 175–200; Stanislav Andreski, *Military Organization and Society* (Berkeley: University of California Press, 1971); Ronald Rogowski, *Commerce and Coalitions: How Trade Affects Domestic Political Alignments*

selection, for example, was not formulated in axiomatic terms, and Darwin could not even specify the full causal mechanism by which favorable traits were passed on to successive generations. Yet the theory was clearly a stunning achievement.[28]

Second, complete logical consistency—and in particular, the ability to deduce testable propositions from a set of general assumptions—is neither necessary nor sufficient for scientific progress. Larry Laudan notes that "inconsistent theories have often been detected in almost all . . . branches of science," and argues that efforts to resolve such inconsistencies often form an important part of specific research traditions.[29] Some evidence even suggests that working scientists routinely ignore the strict canons of logic in their daily work, and are more prone to inferential "errors" than are ordinary citizens.[30]

The social sciences are replete with inconsistent or incomplete but nonetheless highly useful theories. John Maynard Keynes's *General Theory* contains a number of important gaps and inconsistencies (whose exploration dominated the macroeconomic research agenda for several decades), but it was nonetheless a major watershed in economic thought.[31] Similarly, Mancur Olson's *The*

(Princeton, N.J.: Princeton University Press, 1989); John J. Mearsheimer, *Conventional Deterrence* (Ithaca, N.Y.: Cornell University Press, 1983); Robert D. Putnam with Robert Leonardi and Rafaella Y. Nanetti, *Making Democracy Work: Civic Traditions in Modern Italy* (Princeton, N.J.: Princeton University Press, 1993); Robert A. Pape, *Bombing to Win: Air Power and Coercion in War* (Ithaca, N.Y.: Cornell University Press, 1996); Norman H. Nie, Jane Junn, and Ken Stehlik-Berry, *Education and Democratic Citizenship in America* (Chicago: University of Chicago Press, 1997); and Chaim D. Kaufmann, "Out of the Lab and Into the Archives: A Method for Testing Psychological Explanations of Political Decision Making," *International Studies Quarterly*, Vol. 38, No. 4 (December 1994), pp. 557–586.

28. Moreover, Darwinians remained deeply divided over a number of central features of natural selection, such as the inheritability of acquired characteristics. See Robert J. Richards, *Darwin and the Emergence of Evolutionary Theories of Mind and Behavior* (Chicago: University of Chicago Press, 1987).

29. Laudan goes on to say that "the only conceivable response to a conceptual problem of this kind is to refuse to accept the offending theory until the inconsistency is corrected," but he cautions that "the refusal to *accept* an inconsistent theory need not require that one cease working on such a theory." See Laudan, *Progress and Its Problems: Towards a Theory of Scientific Growth* (Berkeley: University of California Press, 1977), pp. 49–50, 230 n. 5 (emphasis in original).

30. Commenting on a study of the psychological traits of scientists, the biologist and philosopher of science David L. Hull points out that "in deductive logic reasoning from 'if p then q' and 'q' to 'p' is fallacious. . . . When scientists and nonscientists were tested, scientists tended to commit this error more frequently than ordinary people. They also tended to reason quite rapidly from minimal data to possible explanations. . . . After all, scientists are involved primarily in nondemonstrative forms of inference, and by definition nondemonstrative inferences fail the canons of deductive logic. *As fallacious as affirming the consequent may be in deductive logic, it is central to science.*" See David L. Hull, *Science as a Process: An Evolutionary Account of the Social and Conceptual Development of Science* (Chicago: University of Chicago Press, 1988), p. 301 (emphasis added).

31. See Marc Trachtenberg, "Keynes Triumphant: A Study of the Social History of Economic Ideas," in Robert Alun Jones and Henrika Kuklick, eds., *Knowledge and Society: Studies in the Sociology of Culture Past and Present* (Greenwich, Conn.: JAI Press, 1983).

Logic of Collective Action contains a number of logical ambiguities, yet is properly regarded as a seminal contribution.[32] In international relations, Kenneth Waltz's *Theory of International Politics* argues that bipolar worlds are stable in part because the two leading powers would compete everywhere and thus reduce the danger of miscalculation. But Waltz also argues that peripheral areas are of little or no strategic consequence, which raises the question of why a rational superpower would compete there in the first place. Despite this contradiction, Waltz's theory has probably been the most influential work in the field over the past two decades, and deservedly so.

These examples suggest that although logical consistency is highly desirable and efforts to achieve it are a central aim of science, it is not the only thing we look for in a theory. Put differently, an incomplete but highly suggestive theory may be an important advance, even if it requires additional work to clarify its deductive logic and identify critical assumptions and boundary conditions.

Logical consistency is also insufficient when a theory's core assumptions are subject to question. Formal rational choice models derive logical conclusions from a set of initial premises about how human beings (or states) make decisions.[33] If human decisions in the real world are not made in the way that rational choice theorists assume, however, then the models may be both deductively consistent and empirically wrong.[34]

For example, many formal models relax the assumption of full information by making additional assumptions about the way each player will revise his or her beliefs.[35] Such models typically assume that actors with incomplete

---

32. For example, Olson argued that small groups are more likely to provide a collective good than are larger groups, based on the claim that each member's share of the good will decline as group size increases, thereby decreasing the individual incentive to contribute. This argument assumes that the collective good is not in "joint supply" (meaning that consumption by one actor does not reduce the amount available to others), and ignores the possibility that certain collective goods (such as the ability to lobby legislators on behalf of some position) may require a large membership to be effective. See Russell Hardin, *Collective Action* (Baltimore, Md.: Johns Hopkins University Press, 1982), chap. 3.

33. A good critique of the utility assumptions common to rational choice theory is Amitai Etzioni, *The Moral Dimension: Toward a New Economics* (New York: Free Press, 1988). I am indebted to Robert Jervis for bringing this source to my attention.

34. Of course, such theories may do a better job of explaining and predicting than do rival theories. This is an empirical issue, however, which is one of the main reasons why it is necessary to subject rational choice models to careful empirical testing.

35. More sophisticated models also make heroic assumptions about the ability of actors to perform complex calculations to determine what course of action to take. This implicit assumption reveals a modest irony: formal modelers are admired because they are able to devise elaborate games and work out increasingly complicated solutions, yet the games themselves are supposed to describe the behavior of ordinary human beings (or collectivities) who have never had a course in game theory and may not even understand simple algebra.

information will revise their initial beliefs according to Bayes's rule, which states how probability estimates are optimally revised in light of new information.[36] Bayes's rule is a principle of probability theory, however, not an empirical law of human decisionmaking. Quite the contrary, in fact, for there is abundant experimental evidence confirming that human beings do not revise their beliefs in this manner.[37] This result means that a formal model in which actors revise their beliefs according to Bayes's rule can be logically consistent but empirically false, because the predictions it generates have been calculated with an empirically inaccurate algorithm.

Another reason why logical consistency is not enough is the well-known problem of "multiple equilibria." Over the past three decades, game theorists have devised ways to build more realistic models by relaxing certain key assumptions (such as the belief that the players have full information). Unfortunately, these more complicated games often contain several equilibrium solutions (i.e., solutions a rational actor would not depart from unilaterally), which means that logical deduction alone cannot tell you which outcome is going to occur.[38] This problem is compounded by the so-called folk theorem,

---

36. Bayes's rule states that the probability that a particular state of the world is true given the occurrence of a particular event is the probability that both the state and the event will occur, divided by the probability that the event will occur independent of the actual state of the world. Formally, if there are two possible states of the world (X and Y), and an event A, Bayes's rule can be written as

$$p(X/A) = \frac{p(X)p(A/X)}{p(X)p(A/X) + p(Y)p(A/Y)} \, .$$

37. See Daniel Kahneman and Amos Tversky, "On the Psychology of Prediction," *Psychological Review*, Vol. 80, No. 4 (July 1973), pp. 237–251; David Grether, "Bayes Rule as a Descriptive Model: The Representativeness Heuristic," *Quarterly Journal of Economics*, Vol. 95, No. 3 (November 1980), pp. 537–557; and Maya Bar-Hillel, "Similarity and Probability," *Organizational Behavior and Human Performance*, Vol. 11, No. 2 (April 1974), pp. 277–282. For general discussions of the rationality assumption in economics, see Robin M. Hogarth and Melvin W. Reder, eds., *Rational Choice: The Contrast between Economics and Psychology* (Chicago: University of Chicago Press, 1987); and Karen Schweers Cook and Margaret Levi, eds., *The Limits of Rationality* (Chicago: University of Chicago Press, 1990). A critical assessment of the use of Bayesian assumptions in game theory is Ken Binmore, "DeBayesing Game Theory," in Binmore, Alan Kirman, and Piero Tani, eds., *Frontiers of Game Theory* (Cambridge, Mass.: MIT Press, 1993).

38. For example, Harrison Wagner's 1992 article on rationality and misperception presents a two-stage game in which a potential challenger is uncertain about the willingness of the defender to retaliate. Wagner shows that there is an equilibrium in which a strong defender always retaliates in the first stage (so as to deter a challenge in stage 2), while a weak deterrer retaliates only occasionally, and the challenger is more likely to be deterred in stage 2. But as Barry O'Neill has pointed out, the model contains another equilibrium in which neither strong nor weak deterrers retaliate in stage 1, and the challenger always challenges in the second. See R. Harrison Wagner, "Rationality and Misperceptions in Deterrence Theory," *Journal of Theoretical Politics*, Vol. 4, No. 2

which says that in repeated games with incomplete information and an appropriate discount for the future payoffs, there are always multiple Nash equilibria.[39] Although it is sometimes possible to identify which equilibria will be preferred—Schelling's famous discussion of "focal points" was an important effort in this area—"formal mathematical game theory has said little or nothing about where these expectations come from."[40]

Within the field of game theory, the main response to the problem of multiple equilibria was to develop more restrictive "solution concepts."[41] A solution concept (such as "Nash equilibrium," "subgame perfect equilibrium," or "perfect Bayesian equilibrium") is a set of restrictions on what a "rational" actor would do. In a formal model of bargaining, for example, a more refined solution concept will eliminate certain equilibria by forbidding players from making logically permissible but otherwise incredible threats, or by placing certain limits on the inferences that players may draw from one another's behavior. By formally restricting certain choices, more refined solution concepts eliminate some of the equilibria and thereby permit more determinate predictions. The problem is that the empirical predictions one draws may depend on the particular solution concept that is employed.[42] Thus more

---

(April 1992), pp. 115–142; and Barry O'Neill, "Are Game Models of Deterrence Biased towards Arms-Building?: Wagner on Rationality and Misperception," *Journal of Theoretical Politics*, Vol. 4, No. 4 (October 1992), pp. 472–473.

39. See Drew Fudenberg and Eric Maskin, "The Folk Theorem in Repeated Games with Discounting or Incomplete Information," *Econometrica*, Vol. 54, No. 3 (May 1986), pp. 533–554.

40. Kreps, *Game Theory and Economic Modelling*, p. 101. The inability of some formal models to identify clear predictions has led some formal theorists to invoke ideas, institutions, or culture as exogenous, ad hoc variables in order to explain which of the various equilibria is chosen. In these accounts, however, the exogenous variables are doing the real work of explaining the outcomes; the game itself is essentially a descriptive framework in which to embed the narrative. See, for example, David Kreps, "Game Theory and Corporate Culture," in Alt and Shepsle, *Perspectives on Positive Political Economy*; Geoffrey Garrett and Barry R. Weingast, "Ideas, Interests, and Institutions: Constructing the European Community's Internal Market," in Judith Goldstein and Robert O. Keohane, eds., *Ideas and Foreign Policy: Beliefs, Institutions, and Political Change* (Ithaca, N.Y.: Cornell University Press, 1993); and Mark Blyth, "'Any More Bright Ideas?': The Ideational Turn in Comparative Political Economy," *Comparative Politics*, Vol. 29, No. 2 (January 1997), pp. 229–250.

41. The search for increasingly refined solution concepts may be going out of fashion among pure game theorists, in part because there is no good way to determine which concepts should be preferred. I am indebted to Michael Chwe for discussion on this point.

42. This point is nicely made in Barry Nalebuff's 1991 article on reputation building. Like the Wagner article just discussed, Nalebuff's model depicts situations where a state is contemplating intervention in one area to deter subsequent interventions elsewhere. The problem is that it is not clear how other actors will interpret different responses. Intervening could be seen as a sign of weakness ("I will intervene now because I cannot meet a later challenge and am therefore trying to bluff"), or it could be seen as a sign of strength ("I will intervene now to demonstrate how strong I am"). The model generates multiple equilibria—for example, there is an equilibrium in

realistic game models can be both logically consistent and indeterminate in the absence of subjective judgments about the particular equilibria the actors are going to prefer.

These criticisms of rational choice theory are not new, and sophisticated game theorists are fully aware of the limitations of the method as well as the strengths. Nor do these difficulties discredit the use of formal models, including such efforts in the field of security studies. But these concerns ought to sound a cautionary note. In game theory, as in life, one rarely gets something for nothing. One can relax the unrealistic assumption of full information, for example, but only at the cost of unrealistic assumptions about the way that actors update beliefs and the ability of real-world decisionmakers to perform complex calculations. Although logical consistency and precision are desirable and formal techniques can help us achieve them, this capacity does not ensure accurate or useful results by itself. By themselves, in short, the potential gains in precision and logical consistency do not demonstrate the superiority of formal techniques over other approaches.

THE COSTS OF FORMALIZATION

Moreover, the potential increase in precision and consistency is bought at a price. Unlike the first wave of formal theorizing, which relied on simple models largely for illustrative purposes, recent formal work has become less and less "user-friendly." Some of the inaccessibility arises from the use of more sophisticated mathematics, but an equally serious barrier is the tendency for many formal theorists to present their ideas in an overly complex and impenetrable manner. In general, formal theorists rely heavily on a specialized jargon and what Donald McCloskey has termed a "scientistic" style, in which formal proofs, lemmas, and propositions are deployed to lend a quasi-scientific patina to otherwise simple ideas.[43] Formal methods also make it easier to bury key assumptions within the model, thereby forcing readers to invest considerable time and effort to unearth the basic logic of the argument.

---

which all states intervene whether they are strong or weak, and another where no states intervene—and Nalebuff goes on to show that the question of whether intervention is "rational" depends on the solution concept that is employed. See Nalebuff, "Rational Deterrence in an Imperfect World," *World Politics*, Vol. 43, No. 3 (April 1991), p. 329.

43. See Donald N. McCloskey, *The Rhetoric of Economics* (Madison: University of Wisconsin Press, 1985); and McCloskey, *Knowledge and Persuasion in Economics* (Cambridge, U.K.: Cambridge University Press, 1994), especially chap. 9.

The obvious defense of increased formalization is simply that this is the price that must be paid for theoretical progress. We do not expect physicists to dumb down superstring theory; by the same logic, one should not expect formal theorists to simplify their work to help other scholars understand it. This argument has some merit. Sophisticated mathematical tools have been of considerable value throughout the social sciences, and one would never want to rule out such techniques a priori. But the increased emphasis on mathematization is not an unalloyed good, particularly if it does not yield a substantial increase in explanatory power.

First, other things being equal, a theory that is easy to grasp and understand is inherently easier to evaluate than one that is impenetrable or obscure. Accessibility increases the number of potential critics, thereby increasing the number of challenges that a theory is likely to face. Facilitating potential challenges contributes to rigor, because the larger the audience that can understand and evaluate a theory, the more likely it is that errors will be exposed and corrected and the better a theory has to be in order to retain approval. By contrast, an incorrect theory that is presented in an opaque or impenetrable way may survive simply because potential critics cannot figure out what the argument is.[44]

Indeed, when a research tradition prizes mathematical rigor above all else, incorrect or trivial ideas may survive because they are presented in a technically impressive way. As Thomas Mayer has written, "With modeling held in such high regard, there is the danger that a trivial idea, if it is accompanied by a large enough bodyguard of equations, will succeed in surmounting the refereeing process. Many published models merely 'algebray' the obvious." Even scholars who have mastered the requisite techniques may be forced "to plough through an elaborate set of equations to get at what could have been said much more briefly."[45]

Second, the time invested learning formal techniques is time that cannot be spent learning a foreign language, mastering the relevant details of an important policy issue, immersing oneself in a new body of theoretical literature, or compiling an accurate body of historical data. Similarly, the time required to

---

44. This principle is not limited to scholarship using mathematics or other technical tools. If qualitative work is written in obscure and inaccessible jargon, or it is based on source materials that are not available to other scholars, this will inhibit critical evaluation and make it easier for dubious work to evade challenge.
45. See Thomas Mayer, *Truth versus Precision in Economics* (Aldershot, U.K.: Edward Elgar, 1993), pp. 123–127.

understand an elaborate formal demonstration (or the time spent perfecting the mathematical details of one's own models) is time that cannot be spent questioning underlying assumptions or testing the empirical validity of the argument. My point is not that these other skills are more valuable than the use of formal techniques, merely that there are opportunity costs involved in relying on any one particular analytic approach.

Finally, a logically consistent and mathematically rigorous theory is of little value if it does not illuminate some important aspect of the real world. As the economist George Stigler (who was hardly opposed to rational choice theory) once commented: "At leading centers of economic theory . . . it has been the practice to ask: Is the new theory logically correct? That is a good question but not as good as the second question: Does the new theory help us to understand observable economic life? . . . Until the second question is answered, a theory has no standing and therefore should not be used as a guide to policy."[46] And even if a formal theory does contribute to scholarly understanding, a forbidding level of technical complexity will make it more difficult for policymakers to use, thereby reducing its practical value.

Once again, these arguments do not imply that formal modeling is not a useful part of the social science toolkit. Rather, they suggest that this research tradition has both strengths and limitations; it imposes costs as well as conferring benefits. The technical complexity of recent formal work might be justified if these techniques led to lots of useful new hypotheses, and if these hypotheses were well supported by careful empirical tests. In other words, if formalization was more likely than other approaches to produce important policy-relevant knowledge, then we might (rationally) disregard these costs. As I shall now show, however, this does not seem to be the case.

Creativity and Originality

Despite the confident claims of some of its practitioners, recent rational choice work in security studies has not produced a noteworthy number of important new theories or hypotheses. Formal rational choice theorists have refined or qualified a number of existing ideas, and they have provided formal treatments of a number of familiar issues. When compared to other research traditions, however, their production of powerful new theories is not very impressive.

---

46. Quoted in ibid., pp. 27–28.

The lack of originality takes two closely related forms. The first form I term "methodological overkill"; the second might be called the problem of "old wine in new bottles." Let us consider each phenomenon in turn, along with some prominent illustrative examples.

METHODOLOGICAL OVERKILL

Methodological overkill refers to the tendency of some elaborate formal models to yield rather trivial theoretical results. Here the problem is not that the arguments are incorrect; rather, the problem is that the elaborate formal machinery does not produce very interesting findings.

EXAMPLE NO. 1. James D. Morrow, "Capabilities, Uncertainty, and Resolve: A Limited Information Model of Crisis Bargaining."[47] This article presents a complex model of crisis bargaining, which assumes that states are uncertain about the balance of power, specific military advantages, and the opponent's resolve. The model is a fairly realistic depiction of some of the factors that influence crisis bargaining, and Morrow also offers some informal tests of the model's predictions.

Unfortunately, Morrow's sophisticated model yields rather trivial results. The central finding is that crises and wars do not arise in the absence of some form of uncertainty, a proposition that has been advanced by a number of other scholars in the past. Morrow also finds that "war is most likely when the initiator's forces are superior to the defender's forces, although war becomes unlikely when the initiator is grossly superior to the defender." The model also reveals that "militarily weak nations are willing to initiate crises when they hold advantages that compensate for their objective military inferiority," and "as the status quo becomes more favorable to the initiator . . . crises and wars become less likely because deterrence is more likely to hold." The model also shows that "the costs of war do discourage the sides from fighting," and suggests that "crises do not occur when the initiator holds strong beliefs that the defender has an advantage, regardless of the true state of affairs" (pp. 956–957, 959). In other words, states do not begin a crisis when they think the other side has a big advantage. There is nothing obviously wrong with these conjectures, but nothing very earth-shattering about them either.

---

47. James D. Morrow, "Capabilities, Uncertainty, and Resolve: A Limited Information Model of Crisis Bargaining," *American Journal of Political Science*, Vol. 33, No. 4 (November 1989), pp. 941–972. Subsequent references to works discussed appear in parentheses in the text.

EXAMPLE NO. 2. Jeffrey S. Banks, "Equilibrium Behavior in Crisis Bargaining Games."[48] This article develops a formal solution to certain bargaining games of incomplete information that is robust with respect to the actual specification of the game. In other words, Banks shows that a certain class of formal results do not depend on the individual features of the game (e.g., the specific number of moves, the order in which the players choose, etc.).

What new hypotheses does the analysis yield? After elaborating a simple two-actor model in which one player possesses private information about the benefits and costs of war, Banks demonstrates that "in any equilibrium of any game with the above format, the probability of war is an increasing function of the expected benefits from war of the informed player." He elaborates: "In any equilibrium of a crisis bargaining game . . . 'stronger' countries (i.e., those with greater expected benefits from war) are more likely to end up in a war; yet if the bargaining negotiations are successful and war is averted, stronger countries receive a better settlement as well" (p. 601). In other words, states that know they will reap greater benefits from war are more likely to enter one; and states with greater power (and greater incentives for war) can strike a better deal when bargaining short of war. Few international relations scholars will find these results surprising, even if one accepts that the model is an accurate representation of real-world crises.[49]

EXAMPLE NO. 3. D. Marc Kilgour and Frank C. Zagare, "Credibility, Uncertainty, and Deterrence."[50] Kilgour and Zagare construct a three-stage formal model of deterrence that is explicitly designed to incorporate uncertainty about each player's willingness to retaliate. The model also allows the players to revise their behavior in light of the opponent's prior conduct. The model and the analysis are fairly sophisticated, but the theoretical and practical results are for the most part affirmations of the conventional wisdom.

Kilgour and Zagare suggest that the "signal contribution" of the model is to provide a "measure of the circumstances in which deterrence can emerge in an uncertain world" (p. 326). The actual results are not very illuminating, however. For example, the authors also find that (1) "the higher each player's evaluation of the . . . status quo, the more likely the sure-thing deterrence equilibrium exists" (p. 321); (2) "deterrence stability is enhanced by increasing

---

48. Jeffrey S. Banks, "Equilibrium Behavior in Crisis Bargaining Games," *American Journal of Political Science*, Vol. 34, No. 3 (August 1990), pp. 599–614.
49. It is worth noting that this article does not offer any empirical support for its claims.
50. D. Marc Kilgour and Frank C. Zagare, "Credibility, Uncertainty, and Deterrence," *American Journal of Political Science*, Vol. 35, No. 2 (May 1991), pp. 305–334.

the costs associated with mutual punishment" (p. 321); and (3) "if at least one player is willing to endure the costs of mutual punishment, deterrence can, but need not, fail" (p. 323). They conclude that "when the credibility of each player's threat is sufficiently high, deterrence is very likely," and further observe that "in core areas, where both players have inherently credible threats, increasing the costs of mutual punishment past a certain point does little to enhance deterrence stability." Given these familiar results, it is not surprising that they recommend "policies of deterrence that are sufficient to inflict unacceptable damage on an opponent yet are survivable enough to be available for a *retaliatory* attack," and that they endorse arms control, single-warhead ICBMs, hardened silos, and other familiar elements of nuclear strategy (pp. 326–327, emphasis in original). In short, Kilgour and Zagare have reinvented the central elements of deterrence theory without improving on it, despite the elaborate formal exercise they perform.[51]

EXAMPLE NO. 4. David Lalman and David Newman, "Alliance Formation and National Security."[52] This article develops an expected utility model of alliance formation and tests it against a body of quantitative data. The analysis is straightforward and clearly presented, but the conclusions are prosaic. For example, the authors find that "nations generally enter into alliances in the expectation of improving their security position," adding that "the pattern of alliance formation through time is related to the opportunity to enhance security . . . *realpolitik* considerations of security are crucial to alliance formation decisions" (p. 251). Although the analysis itself is careful and straightforward, it is not clear what has been gained from formalization.

EXAMPLE NO. 5. James D. Morrow, "Alliances, Credibility, and Peacetime Costs."[53] This article presents a sophisticated game-theoretic model in which alliances are a means of signaling interests in the presence of uncertainty. Although Morrow's formulation challenges the idea that alliance credibility is largely driven by concerns about reputation, the conclusions for the most part

---

51. Interestingly, Kilgour and Zagare's model produces results different from Morrow's model described above. Morrow's central finding was the impossibility of war in the absence of some form of uncertainty, whereas Kilgour and Zagare find that "misperception is neither necessary nor sufficient for the failure of mutual deterrence." Ibid., p. 317. Among other things, this shows that modeling alone does not ensure truth, as one can create a model to produce any particular conclusion that one might want.
52. David Lalman and David Newman, "Alliance Formation and National Security," *International Interactions*, Vol. 16, No. 4 (1991), pp. 239–254.
53. James D. Morrow, "Alliances, Credibility, and Peacetime Costs," *Journal of Conflict Resolution*, Vol. 38, No. 2 (June 1994), pp. 270–297.

echo the conventional wisdom. In particular, the model implies that (1) "tighter alliances improve the ability of allies to fight together while imposing higher peacetime costs," and (2) "tighter alliances tend to produce greater deterrence and a higher probability of intervention (on behalf of one's ally)." This is probably correct but neither surprising nor counterintuitive, and Morrow himself notes that "the implications of the model appear to be consistent with stylized facts about alliances" (p. 294).

In each of these examples, in short, technical sophistication and logical consistency did not yield particularly creative or original results.

OLD WINE IN NEW BOTTLES

In addition to producing rather trivial results, formal models sometimes use new concepts or labels for familiar ideas, so what at first glance seems like a wholly original contribution turns out to be an old argument in a slightly different guise.[54] Consider the following examples.

EXAMPLE NO. 6. Robert Powell, "Absolute and Relative Gains in International Relations Theory."[55] This article presents a simple formal model showing how the willingness of states to cooperate is affected by the distribution of benefits. The argument is simple and consistent with familiar realist logic: states worry more about the distribution of benefits when they fear that others might use their share of the gains to increase their military power and attack. As this fear increases, incentives to cooperate will decline.

Although Powell's specification of the problem is an improvement over earlier treatments (including the seminal work of Joseph Grieco), the basic argument is an old one.[56] In Powell's model, the critical variable that determines the prospects for cooperation is "the technology of warfare." In his words, "If the use of force is at issue because the cost of fighting is sufficiently low, cooperation collapses. . . . But if the use of force is no longer at issue,

---

54. Needless to say, formal theorists are not the only social scientists who engage in this practice.
55. Robert Powell, "Absolute and Relative Gains in International Relations Theory," *American Political Science Review*, Vol. 85, No. 4 (December 1991), pp. 1303–1320.
56. Grieco distinguished between two types of states with different preferences: those that cared about "relative" gains (which he called "defensive positionalists") and those that did not (or "rational egoists"). By contrast, Powell assumes that all states have similar preferences, but their behavior varies with the external constraints they face. This formulation is simpler and more consistent with realist premises than Grieco's. See Joseph Grieco, "Anarchy and the Limits of Cooperation," in David Baldwin, ed., *Neorealism and Neoliberalism: The Contemporary Debate* (New York: Columbia University Press, 1993); Grieco, *Cooperation among Nations: Europe, America, and the Non-Tariff Barriers to Trade* (Ithaca, N.Y.: Cornell University Press, 1990); and Robert Powell, "The Neorealist-Neoliberal Debate," *International Organization*, Vol. 48, No. 2 (Spring 1994), especially pp. 334–338.

cooperation again becomes feasible" (p. 1311). What Powell calls the "technology of warfare," however, is essentially identical to the concept of the offense-defense balance identified by George Quester, Robert Jervis, and Stephen Van Evera. As Jervis put it back in 1978: "If the defense has enough of an advantage . . . , the security dilemma [will] cease to inhibit status quo states from cooperating."[57] This is identical to Powell's claim that cooperation becomes more likely as the technology of warfare makes using force more costly (which implies that defenders can inflict high costs on attackers). Powell's article is a useful contribution to the absolute/relative gains debate, but it does not make a fundamentally new argument.

EXAMPLE NO. 7. James D. Fearon, "Rationalist Theories of War."[58] This article presents a rationalist framework for understanding the outbreak of war, using a simple formal bargaining model. Given the plausible assumption that fighting is always costly, Fearon argues that a satisfactory rationalist theory of war has to explain why the parties involved could not reach the same outcome via negotiation, thereby avoiding the costs of war.[59]

According to Fearon, the theoretical existence of outcomes that rational states should prefer to war implies that war can arise in only one of two ways. First, war arises because states have "private information" about power and resolve *and* powerful incentives to lie about it. They may misrepresent their strength or resolve to try to gain a better deal in a given confrontation, but this tactic may also lead them to overlook a negotiated solution that would have been preferable to war. Second, war can result from what he calls the "commitment problem." Even if both sides may know that a satisfactory bargain exists, they cannot accept the deal because they cannot be sure that it will be kept.

This article is useful because it suggests that rationalist theories of war are really of only two kinds, and it identifies how rational states can end up fighting even when there are negotiated solutions that each prefers to war.[60] But the central argument—that wars arise either from the "commitment prob-

---

57. See Jervis, "Cooperation under the Security Dilemma," p. 187.
58. James D. Fearon, "Rationalist Theories of War," *International Organization,* Vol. 49, No. 3 (Summer 1995), pp. 379–414.
59. The logic of this argument is similar to the theory of industrial disputes advanced by John Hicks in the 1930s. In Hicks's case, the question is why labor and management cannot reach agreement on a contract solely via negotiation, thereby avoiding the costs of a strike. See Hicks, *The Theory of Wages* (London: Macmillan, 1932), chap. 7.
60. Fearon's argument applies only to the final decision to wage war, once there is a concrete dispute between two states. It does not address the other conditions that might operate to make war more likely, such as ideological differences, shifting balances of power, the perceived weakness of a particular regime, or the domestic incentives that might drive a particular regime to seek war for its own sake.

lem" or "private information"—is not new. What Fearon calls the "commitment problem" (a term borrowed from recent formal work in economics) has long been recognized as a central feature of international anarchy. As Robert Art and Robert Jervis put it in 1976: "International politics takes place in an arena that has no central authority. . . . *States can make commitments and treaties, but no sovereign power ensures compliance.*" Similarly, Kenneth Oye noted in 1986 that because "states cannot cede ultimate control over their conduct to a supranational sovereign, *they cannot guarantee they will adhere to their promises.*"[61] Thus, to say that war arises from the "commitment problem" is merely to give a new label to a well-established idea.

In addition, although the concept of "private information" is broader than the more familiar idea of "secrecy," its effects on crisis bargaining are essentially the same.[62] It is not a new idea to claim that states are more likely to miscalculate when their opponents conceal information from them, although it is important to distinguish this source of miscalculation from errors arising from cognitive or organizational sources of misperception (a task Fearon accomplishes very well). Thus, although Fearon's analysis clarifies these issues in an insightful and intelligent way, the formalization does not yield a new theoretical claim.[63]

EXAMPLE NO. 8. "Costly Signals" and Reputation Building. A similar conclusion emerges when we examine the formal literature on reputation, and especially its reliance on the idea of "costly signaling."[64] The basic claim of these

---

61. See Robert Art and Robert Jervis, "Introduction," in Art and Jervis, *International Politics*, 1st ed. (Boston: Little, Brown, 1976), p. 2 (emphasis added); and Kenneth A. Oye, ed., *Cooperation under Anarchy* (Princeton, N.J.: Princeton University Press, 1985), p. 1 (emphasis added).

62. Unlike some forms of secrecy (such as number of weapons, for example), "private information" includes information (such as a player's level of resolve) that could not be reliably revealed to the other side even if one wanted to.

63. Fearon's discussion of "rationalist" theories does not explain when war will or will not occur. As he notes at the end of the article, both the problem of "private information" and the "commitment problem" created by anarchy are constant features of international politics and thus cannot explain why war occurs in some circumstances but not in others. See Fearon, "Rationalist Theories of War," p. 410.

64. Of this large and growing literature, see especially Reinhard Selten, "The Chain-Store Paradox," *Theory and Decision*, Vol. 9, No. 2 (April 1978), pp. 127–159; David M. Kreps, Paul Milgrom, John Roberts, and Robert Wilson, "Rational Cooperation in the Finitely Repeated Prisoners' Dilemma," pp. 245–252; Kreps and Wilson, "Reputation and Imperfect Information," pp. 253–279; and Milgrom and Roberts, "Predation, Reputation, and Entry Deterrence," pp. 280–312. All appear in *Journal of Economic Theory*, Vol. 27, No. 2 (August 1982). See also Wilson, "Deterrence in Oligopolistic Competition," in Stern et al., *Perspectives on Deterrence;* and Wilson, "Reputations in Games and Markets," in Alvin E. Roth, *Game-Theoretic Models of Bargaining* (Cambridge, U.K.: Cambridge University Press, 1985).

models is straightforward: because an actor's true preferences are unobservable and talk is cheap, an actor can signal its true preferences only by employing a "costly signal." Such signals are actions that impose higher costs on an actor with low resolve, and thus are more likely to be made only by actors who are more resolute. A number of formal theorists have used this concept in interesting ways, but the basic idea is virtually identical to Robert Jervis's distinction between "signals" and "indices," which he laid out more than twenty-five years ago.[65] As Jervis puts it, "Signals can be as easily issued by a deceiver as by an honest actor . . . they do not contain inherent credibility." By contrast, indices (which is Jervis's term for costly signals) "are statements or actions that carry some inherent evidence that the image projected is correct." Specifically, "behavior that is felt to be too important or costly in its own right to be used for other ends is an index."[66]

Again, the point is not that the formal literature on costly signaling has added nothing to our understanding of international politics. Rather, my point is that the idea that reputations could rest on what are now called "costly signals" did not emerge from a formal analysis. Accordingly, this literature cannot be used as evidence that formal theory is a superior source of new concepts or hypotheses. Formalization has refined our understanding, perhaps, but even that claim has not gone unchallenged.[67]

Taken together, these examples reveal that even sophisticated formal analyses often lead to familiar conclusions about the behavior of states. Does this mean that formal theory has added nothing new? Of course not. Schelling's early work was extremely influential, as was the application of collective goods theory to the question of alliance burden-sharing.[68] Robert Axelrod's analysis of the logic of cooperation in an iterated prisoner's dilemma has had a far-

---

65. Examples include Nalebuff, "Rational Deterrence in an Imperfect World"; Wagner, "Rationality and Misperception in Deterrence"; D. Marc Kilgour, "Domestic Political Structure and War Behavior: A Game-Theoretic Approach," *Journal of Conflict Resolution*, Vol. 35, No. 2 (June 1991), pp. 266–284; and Andrew Kydd, "Game Theory and the Spiral Model," *World Politics*, Vol. 49, No. 3 (April 1997), pp. 371–400.
66. See Robert Jervis, *The Logic of Images in International Relations* (Princeton, N.J.: Princeton University Press, 1970), pp. 21, 26. For a discussion of the relationship between his early work and recent economic work on reputation, see Jervis, "Drawing Inferences and Projecting Images," paper presented at the annual meeting of the International Studies Association, San Diego, California, April 1996.
67. For a fair-minded critique of the formal literature on reputation, see Jonathan Mercer, *Reputation and International Politics* (Ithaca, N.Y.: Cornell University Press, 1996), pp. 28–42.
68. The seminal piece is Mancur Olson and Richard Zeckhauser, "An Economic Theory of Alliances," *Review of Economics and Statistics*, Vol. 48, No. 2 (August 1966), pp. 266–279.

reaching impact in many areas, including the study of strategy.[69] Recent formal work has also shown how certain phenomena (such as the stability of an arms control agreement) can be sensitive to the level of information available to the actors, and formal analysis can increase our confidence in an existing theory by confirming its logical soundness.[70] So the criticisms noted above should not be interpreted as a blanket condemnation either of formalization in general or of its recent manifestations in security studies.[71]

Yet it should also be clear that formal theory enjoys no particular advantage as a source of theoretical creativity.[72] In addition to confining the analysis to an individualistic, rational actor framework, the technical requirements of modern game theory tend to shape both the topics that are chosen and the ways they are addressed. It is not surprising, for example, that much of the formal work in security studies focuses on two-party interactions (and especially on crisis behavior), because these situations are mathematically tractable. This tendency makes good methodological sense, but it may also help explain why other approaches have been more theoretically fruitful, and have made more useful contributions to other security problems.

---

69. Strictly speaking, Axelrod's results emerged from a computer simulation rather than from a formal model. His argument rests on the logic of the iterated prisoner's dilemma, however, and helps highlight the importance of these games for the formal analysis of cooperation. Given that some parts of Axelrod's argument did not stand up to careful formal scrutiny, this example also supports the claim that creativity and theoretical fertility are more important than strict logical consistency. See Robert Axelrod, *The Evolution of Cooperation* (New York: Basic Books, 1984).

70. See George Downs and David Rocke, *Tacit Bargaining and Arms Control* (Ann Arbor: University of Michigan Press, 1989); and Downs and Rocke, *Optimal Imperfection?: Domestic Uncertainty and Institutions in International Relations* (Princeton, N.J.: Princeton University Press, 1995).

71. For a nuanced appreciation of the contributions and limitations of rational choice theorizing, see James B. Rule, *Theory and Progress in Social Science* (Cambridge, U.K.: Cambridge University Press, 1997), chap. 3.

72. It is worth noting that some of the most interesting and important theoretical innovations in security studies over the past two decades have come from nonformal theorists. For example, John Steinbruner and Bruce Blair made a major contribution to deterrence theory by highlighting the importance of organizational and operational considerations; Robert Jervis offered a comprehensive inventory of the ways that psychological biases could affect foreign policy decisionmakers; John Mearsheimer developed and tested a simple theory of conventional deterrence; Barry Posen showed how external conditions and organization theory could explain key elements of great power military doctrine; and Robert Pape constructed and tested a theory of military coercion. More recently, scholars like Peter Katzenstein, Elizabeth Kier, and Alastair Iain Johnston have applied cultural and constructivist approaches to security studies, all of them based on extensive empirical work. One need not be persuaded by all of these works to recognize that they were important efforts to bring social science to bear on important security problems. For a useful survey, see Richard K. Betts, "Should Strategic Studies Survive?" *World Politics*, Vol. 50, No. 1 (October 1997), pp. 7–33.

Furthermore, the history of both natural and social science suggests that theoretical innovations emerge not from abstract modeling exercises, but primarily from efforts to solve concrete empirical puzzles. Indeed, simple observation and largely atheoretical experimentation can be as important as subsequent efforts to devise a deductive structure to explain the observations.[73] In other words, induction and deduction are equally valid avenues for creating a theory, and the former may in fact be more fruitful.

Deterrence theory offers an obvious example. Contrary to the traditional view, formal theory played no role in the creation of deterrence theory.[74] Rather, it emerged largely from Bernard Brodie's historically informed speculations and from Albert Wohlstetter's famous RAND study on the optimal location for U.S. bomber bases. A similar example is the initial development of the bureaucratic politics paradigm by Andrew Marshall and Joseph Loftus, who were trying to account for apparently irrational Soviet military allocations.[75] Among other things, these episodes confirm that case studies can be an extremely fertile source of new theories as well as a useful way to test both formal and nonformal theories.[76]

The bottom line is that although formal approaches to security affairs have produced a number of interesting refinements, the overall level of theoretical innovation is not superior to other social scientific methods. Formalization can impart greater precision and help identify inconsistencies or qualifications, but it enjoys no particular advantage as a source of new hypotheses.

Empirical Validity

The ultimate measure of a theory is its ability to explain real events in the real world. As Maurice Allais warned in his address accepting the Nobel Prize for economics, "Mere logical, even mathematical deduction remains worthless in

---

73. See Ian Hacking, *Representing and Intervening: Introductory Topics in the Philosophy of Natural Science* (New York: Cambridge University Press, 1983), pp. 154–158, 248–249; and Stephen Toulmin, *Human Understanding*, Volume 1: *The Collective Use and Evolution of Concepts* (Princeton, N.J.: Princeton University Press, 1972), pp. 189–190.
74. On this point, see O'Neill, "Game Theory Models of War and Peace," pp. 1010–1013.
75. See Bernard Brodie, ed., *The Absolute Weapon: Atomic Power and World Order* (New York: Harcourt, Brace, 1946); A.J. Wohlstetter, F.S. Hoffman, R.J. Lutz, and H.S. Rowen, *Selection and Use of Strategic Air Bases*, RAND Report P-266 (Santa Monica, Calif.: RAND, 1962); and Marc Trachtenberg, *History and Strategy* (Princeton, N.J.: Princeton University Press, 1991), pp. 29–31.
76. On the latter point, see Bruce Russett, "International Behavior Research: Case Studies and Cumulation," in Russett, *Power and Community in World Politics* (San Francisco, Calif.: W.H. Freeman, 1974), pp. 16–17.

terms of an understanding of reality if it is not closely linked to that reality. . . . Any theory whatever, if it is not verified by empirical evidence, has no scientific value and should be rejected."[77] A research tradition that insists on careful and systematic empirical testing is setting a higher standard for itself than one that places relatively little value on the provision of empirical support. Mere logical consistency is not sufficient.

Does recent rational choice scholarship in security studies pay sufficient attention to this criterion? The answer is no. With a few notable exceptions, the bulk of formal work in security affairs does not engage in any empirical testing at all. Anecdotes and "stylized facts" are sometimes used to explicate a point and to enhance the plausibility of the argument, but relatively little effort is devoted to rigorous empirical evaluation.[78] Other formalists have used mathematical simulations or referred to supportive quantitative evidence, but

---

77. Quoted in Mayer, *Truth versus Precision in Economics*, p. 27. Albert Einstein shared this view. He praised Johannes Kepler for recognizing that "even the most lucidly logical mathematical theory was of itself no guarantee of truth, becoming meaningless unless it was checked against the most exacting observations in natural science." And Einstein called Galileo Galilei "the father of modern physics" because Galileo realized that "pure logical thinking cannot yield us any knowledge of the empirical world. . . . Propositions arrived at by purely logical means are completely empty as regards reality." Quoted in Timothy Ferris, *The Whole Shebang: A State of the Universe(s) Report* (New York: Touchstone, 1997), p. 28. Gary King, Robert Keohane, and Sidney Verba offer a similar appraisal, writing that "formal models do not constitute verified explanations without empirical evaluation of their predictions." See King, Keohane, and Verba, *Designing Social Inquiry: Scientific Inference in Qualitative Research* (Princeton, N.J.: Princeton University Press, 1994), pp. 105–106.

78. For example, the following formal works contain no empirical evidence, and rely entirely on formal deduction: Powell, *Nuclear Deterrence Theory;* Powell, "Absolute and Relative Gains in International Relations Theory"; Powell, "Guns, Butter, and Anarchy," *American Political Science Review,* Vol. 87, No. 1 (March 1993), pp. 115–132; Powell, "Stability and the Distribution of Power," *World Politics,* Vol. 48, No. 2 (January 1996), pp. 239–267; Fearon, "Rationalist Theories of War"; Banks, "Equilibrium Behavior in Crisis Bargaining Games"; James D. Morrow, "A Spatial Model of International Conflict," *American Political Science Review,* Vol. 80, No. 4 (December 1986), pp. 1131–1150; R. Harrison Wagner, "Deterrence and Bargaining," *Journal of Conflict Resolution,* Vol. 26, No. 2 (June 1982), pp. 329–358; Wagner, "Rationality and Misperception in Deterrence"; Wagner, "Nuclear Deterrence, Counterforce Strategies, and the Incentive to Strike First," *American Political Science Review,* Vol. 85, No. 3 (September 1991), pp. 727–749; Kilgour and Zagare, "Credibility, Uncertainty, and Deterrence"; Kilgour, "Domestic Political Structure and War Behavior"; Morrow, "Alliances, Credibility, and Peacetime Costs"; Nalebuff, "Rational Deterrence in an Imperfect World"; Nalebuff, "Minimal Nuclear Deterrence," *Journal of Conflict Resolution,* Vol. 32, No. 3 (September 1988); Nalebuff, "Brinkmanship and Nuclear Deterrence: The Neutrality of Escalation," *Conflict Management and Peace Science,* Vol. 9, No. 2 (Spring 1986), pp. 19–30; Alasdair Smith, "Diversionary Foreign Policy in Democratic Systems," *International Studies Quarterly,* Vol. 40, No. 1 (March 1996), pp. 133–153; Smith, "Alliance Formation and War," *International Studies Quarterly,* Vol. 39, No. 4 (December 1995), pp. 405–425; Smith, "International Crises and Domestic Politics," *American Political Science Review,* Vol. 92, No. 3 (September 1998), pp. 623–638; and Kydd, "Game Theory and the Spiral Model."

these approaches fall short of a careful empirical test.[79] Empirical testing is not a central part of the formal theory enterprise—at least, not in the subfield of security studies—and probably constitutes its most serious limitation.[80]

EXAMPLE NO. 9. James D. Fearon, "Domestic Audience Costs and the Escalation of International Disputes."[81] The limitations that arise from the low priority placed upon empirical testing are nicely revealed in James Fearon's formal analysis of domestic audience costs and crisis bargaining. Fearon's argument is intuitively plausible, technically sophisticated, and informed by his knowledge of international history. Fearon goes to some lengths to identify the real-world implications of his analysis, and the article is in many ways an exemplary use of the formal approach.

Fearon defines audience costs as the domestic political osts that leaders incur when they back down in a crisis. Using a simple bargaining model in which leaders of different states face different audience costs, he finds that once a crisis is under way, "the side with a stronger domestic audience (e.g., a democracy) is always less likely to back down than the side less able to generate audience costs (a nondemocracy)." He also suggests that the constraints imposed by audience costs may explain why democratic states are less prone to conflict with each other; specifically, the presence of high audience costs allows democratic leaders to signal their intentions more credibly, thereby minimizing the miscalculations that can lead to war (pp. 577, 586).[82]

---

79. Examples of these approaches to testing include Jean-Pierre Langlois, "Rational Deterrence and Crisis Stability," *American Journal of Political Science*, Vol. 35, No. 4 (November 1991), pp. 801–832; Downs and Rocke, *Tacit Bargaining and Arms Control;* Downs and Rocke, *Optimal Imperfection?;* and Morrow, "Capabilities, Uncertainty, and Resolve."
80. Between 1989 and 1998, for example, *World Politics* published twelve articles that contained a formal model. Of these, only five contained systematic empirical evidence. The *Journal of Conflict Resolution* published thirty-seven formal articles in the same period (excluding articles dealing solely with technical aspects of game theory), of which thirteen contained empirical support for the model. *International Studies Quarterly* contained twenty-six formal articles in this period, but only ten contained empirical evidence, and *International Organization* published fourteen, seven of which provided empirical support for the model. Overall, roughly 60 percent of these articles relied solely on formal deduction and anecdotal illustration, rather than systematic empirical testing. Similarly, a total of ninety-four formal theory manuscripts were submitted to the *American Political Science Review* between August 1996 and August 1997, but only twenty-five of them (26 percent) contained systematic empirical evidence. See Finifter, "Report of the Editor of the *APSR*," p. 784.
81. James D. Fearon, "Domestic Audience Costs and the Escalation of International Disputes," *American Political Science Review*, Vol. 88, No. 3 (September 1994), pp. 577–592.
82. The idea that relative audience costs will affect bargaining power is not new. As far as I know, the idea was first articulated by Thomas Schelling, who also suggested that democratic and nondemocratic states might differ on this dimension. See Schelling, *Strategy of Conflict*, pp. 27–29.

What is not clear is whether the argument is in fact correct. To begin with, Fearon's model assumes that democracies typically face greater domestic audience costs than nondemocracies, and that both democratic and nondemocratic leaders recognize that this is the case. If an authoritarian regime *believed* that its own audience costs were higher (e.g., due to the fear of a coup or because the regime thought that democratic publics were easily manipulated), the model's predictions would not hold.[83] Yet Fearon offers only anecdotal evidence that authoritarian states actually face lower audience costs, or that this belief is widely shared by democratic and nondemocratic leaders.[84]

Second, the model also assumes that leaders and publics hold similar preferences about the proper course of action. Domestic audiences will punish leaders who back down, but they may also reward a leader who overreaches at first and then manages to retreat short of war. Thus the British and French governments did not suffer domestic audience costs when they backed down during the Rhineland crisis of 1936 or the Munich crisis in 1938, because public opinion did not support going to war.[85]

Third, although Fearon does present some illustrative anecdotes and refers to several quantitative studies that are consistent with his argument, he does not test the logic of the model directly.[86] And it is not difficult to think of possible exceptions: (1) the United States gave in to North Korea's demands following the seizure of the *Pueblo* in 1968 and also granted many of Iran's demands following the seizure of the U.S. embassy in 1980, even though it

---

83. The personal cost to a deposed tyrant could be higher on average than the cost to a democratic incumbent who risks losing the next election, and authoritarian leaders often face other domestic pressures that limit their ability to back down once a crisis is under way. For example, the belief that the Hapsburg monarchy faced internal revolt unless it eliminated the threat from Serbia drove Austro-Hungarian decisions in the July crisis that led to World War I, and the three authoritarian states involved in the July crisis (Germany, Austria-Hungary, and Russia) were clearly less willing to compromise than were democratic Britain and France.
84. As Fearon notes, "The idea that democratic leaders on average have an easier time generating audience costs is advanced here as a plausible working hypothesis." See Fearon, "Domestic Audience Costs," p. 582.
85. A further complication arises if neither leaders nor publics know how resolved they are until *after* the crisis is under way. As a result, a particular leader may adopt a hard-line position at first, based on the belief that it is in the "objective" interest of the state and that this position has popular backing. As the crisis continues, however, the citizenry may become alarmed by the danger of war and eager for a peaceful resolution. A democratic leader who backed down at this point might be rewarded rather than penalized, whereas a leader who continued to escalate might be punished for adventurism.
86. A recent quantitative study that supports some of Fearon's predictions is Joe Eyerman and Robert A. Hart, Jr., "An Empirical Test of the Audience Cost Proposition: Democracy Speaks Louder Than Words," *Journal of Conflict Resolution*, Vol. 40, No. 4 (December 1996), pp. 597–616.

probably faced higher audience costs than did North Korea or Iran; (2) Britain, France, and Israel backed down to U.S. (and possibly Soviet) pressure following the Suez War in 1956, even though their "audience costs" were much higher than those of their opponents;[87] (3) higher "audience costs" did not enable the United States to prevail against England in the *Trent* affair in 1861, and public opinion had virtually no impact in the Venezuelan crisis in 1895–96;[88] and (4) domestic audience costs were dwarfed by other considerations prior to the Six-Day War in 1967 and the War of Attrition in 1969–70.[89]

Fourth, the absence of empirical testing is also important because the model omits another potentially important determinant of crisis behavior. For some states (including some democracies), the principal cost of backing down in a crisis may not be domestic censure but the fear that allies may defect and that adversaries will be emboldened. If there is a sharp difference in the *external* audience costs that each state faces, then a difference in *domestic* audience costs may fade into insignificance.[90] This question is ultimately an empirical one, of course, and cannot be resolved by a purely formal analysis.

In short, this article offers an interesting and intuitively plausible conjecture about crisis bargaining, one well worth further exploration. Until it is rigorously tested, however, there is no way of knowing how significant the actual contribution really is.

---

87. Robert A. Pape argues that Soviet nuclear threats played a critical role in convincing British leaders to withdraw from Egypt after the Suez invasion, but other scholars have reached different conclusions. See Pape, "Why Economic Sanctions Do Not Work," *International Security*, Vol. 22, No. 2 (Fall 1997), pp. 115–117; and James G. Richter, *Khrushchev's Double Bind: International Pressures and Domestic Coalition Politics* (Baltimore, Md.: Johns Hopkins University Press, 1994), p. 93.

88. See Christopher Layne, "Kant or Cant: The Myth of the Democratic Peace," *International Security*, Vol. 19, No. 2 (Fall 1994), pp. 5–49.

89. Israel's decision to preempt in 1967 is consistent with Fearon's model, insofar as the model suggests that democracies will escalate more readily once a crisis is under way. But domestic audience costs did not play a key role in either state's decisions to escalate the crisis or in the final decision to go to war. Both Egypt and Israel seem to have been equally resolute, in part because both believed they were ready for war. Nasser's reluctance to back down was based in part on his concerns about *external* audience costs (and especially the loss of prestige in the Arab world), which underscores the unimportance of relative *domestic* costs in this case. Similarly, nondemocratic Egypt gained a tactical victory over democratic Israel during the 1969–70 War of Attrition, in part because Israeli resolve waned as the conflict continued and in part because the fear of escalation led the superpowers to impose terms that were favorable to Egypt. See Jonathan Shimshoni, *Israel and Conventional Deterrence: Border Warfare from 1953 to 1970* (Ithaca, N.Y.: Cornell University Press, 1988), pp. 169–171.

90. These concerns are not unrelated, of course, because failure to preserve one's external reputation is one reason why a domestic audience might seek to remove a particular leader. Nonetheless, the two concerns are conceptually and empirically distinct.

TAKING TESTING SERIOUSLY?

When formal theorists do engage in extensive empirical testing, moreover, the tests themselves are not as "rigorous" as they might initially appear. To illustrate this point, let us consider two ambitious attempts to combine formal analysis with extensive empirical testing: (1) Bruce Bueno de Mesquita and David Lalman, *War and Reason: Domestic and International Imperatives,* and (2) Emerson M.S. Niou, Peter C. Ordeshook, and Gregory F. Rose, *The Balance of Power: Stability in International Systems.* I have chosen these works because their authors emphasize the importance of testing theories empirically, and because both have been seen as salient demonstrations of the power of formal theory.[91] The question is how rigorous are the tests and how well do the theories perform?

EXAMPLE NO. 10. Bruce Bueno de Mesquita and David Lalman, *War and Reason: Domestic and International Imperatives.*[92] The centerpiece of *War and Reason* is a formal model with two players (state A and state B) and eight possible outcomes: the status quo (SQ), negotiation (N), capitulation by A (Cap$_A$), capitulation by B (Cap$_B$), war begun by A (War$_A$), war begun by B (War$_B$), acquiescence by A (Acq$_A$), and acquiescence by B (Acq$_B$). They make a number of general assumptions about state preferences and assume that all states act to maximize their expected utility. The bulk of the subsequent analysis explores the additional restrictions (e.g., on the domestic costs of using force, the cost of giving in after being attacked, etc.) that would make each outcome the "equilibrium" outcome. These additional assumptions are then interpreted as the underlying conditions that yield each outcome in the game.[93]

---

91. For example, Frank Zagare's review of *War and Reason* in the *American Political Science Review,* Vol. 87, No. 3 (September 1993), p. 811, praised it as "the most significant application to date of game theory to the question of war and peace," and Glenn Snyder called *The Balance of Power* "a valuable, ground-breaking effort" that "blazes a useful trail." See Snyder, "Alliances, Balance, and Stability," *International Organization,* Vol. 43, No. 1 (Winter 1991), pp. 140, 142.
92. Bruce Bueno de Mesquita and David Lalman, *War and Reason: Domestic and International Imperatives* (New Haven, Conn.: Yale University Press, 1992).
93. As with some of the other formal work discussed above, many of the results derived from the model are rather trivial. After deriving and testing more than twenty hypotheses, for example, Bueno de Mesquita and Lalman offer the following general conclusions: "To state it crudely: national leaders wage war when the expected gains minus the expected costs of doing so outweigh the net expected consequences of alternative choices. War can be stumbled into when one nation judges the intentions of a rival too optimistically. War can begin even with full information if it is motivated by a fear of ceding any advantage that is attached to the first use of force. The anticipated net gains from war may be real and tangible acquisitions, or they may be the avoidance of a future expected to be worse than the one anticipated through warfare." They also find that war will not occur if two states prefer negotiation to using force, and if both sides know this with 100 percent confidence. In other words, if both sides would rather talk than fight and if both sides know this, they do not fight. See Bueno de Mesquita and Lalman, *War and Reason,* p. 250.

The predictions derived from the model are tested with a series of large-*N* analyses and a number of briefer case studies. At first glance, these tests appear to show overwhelming success for the model. Upon closer examination, however, the results are not compelling and do not achieve a high level of rigor.

Bueno de Mesquita and Lalman offer numerous statistical tests of their various hypotheses, based on a data set of 707 dyadic relationships between European states from 1815 to 1970.[94] Although they do not describe their statistical procedures in much detail (which makes it difficult to evaluate their conclusions), the results appear to provide convincing support for the model.[95] Unfortunately, there are at least three noteworthy problems with their statistical tests.

First, the quantitative indicators they employ face severe problems of internal validity, given the intrinsic difficulty of obtaining valid quantitative indicators for concepts like "risk propensity," "utility," and "uncertainty," and then applying them to 707 dyads going back to 1815. To their credit, Bueno de Mesquita and Lalman recognize the difficulty of the task and admit that their indicators are quite crude (p. 280). Unfortunately, this also means that the quantitative tests are not very rigorous, because the indicators on which they are based do not adequately capture the theoretical relationships set forth in the formal model.

Second, the statistical tests are compromised by the lack of precise measures for key variables in the model. As they admit, Bueno de Mesquita and Lalman were unable to devise measures for some of the critical variables in the equilibrium conditions that yield different outcomes. The practical result of these missing conditions is that events they code as consistent with a particular outcome may be equally consistent with several other outcomes, which means that the tests blend successful and unsuccessful predictions. Thus we do not know how many successful predictions the model actually makes.

Even if this problem were corrected, Bueno de Mesquita and Lalman's specific testing procedure exaggerates their model's performance. In particular,

94. Specifically, their data set consists of 469 events in which two states engaged in a dispute with each other, plus another 238 observations on randomly paired dyads, included to represent the "nonevents" that are often excluded from quantitative studies. Thus the analysis is based on 707 dyad observations.
95. To note one example, on p. 84 they describe a dummy variable labeled BACQ, which is meant to satisfy the theoretical conditions of Proposition 3.5 (the "acquiescence by B theorem"). The reader is told that "the details of the operationalization are in appendix 1," but there is in fact no mention of this dummy variable anywhere in the appendix and only a very general discussion of the actual measures they employed. The reader is also referred to a number of earlier articles and books for explanations of key elements of the methodology, thereby making it even more difficult to figure out what they have done.

although their model contains eight possible outcomes, most of the hypotheses are tested by constructing a 2×2 table of observed and predicted outcomes, asking simply whether or not the predicted outcome occurred. Unfortunately, collapsing eight categories into two lumps together cases where a particular outcome was predicted and actually occurred and any cases where a particular outcome was predicted but did not occur, thereby generating inflated chi-squared and goodness of fit statistics.[96] Taken together, these flaws undermine their otherwise laudable effort to test the model through a detailed quantitative analysis.

One response to these problems would be to supplement the quantitative analyses with case studies, where one could hope to obtain more valid and reliable measures of key variables.[97] Ideally, a detailed process-tracing of an appropriate set of case studies would have allowed the authors to determine if the participants in interstate crises made choices in the manner depicted by the model, thereby providing a more convincing demonstration of its explanatory power. Unfortunately, the case studies contained in *War and Reason* do not provide this sort of evidence and do not achieve a high standard of rigor. Consider the following three examples.

The Fashoda Crisis. In chapter 3 of *War and Reason*, Bueno de Mesquita and Lalman deduce Proposition 3.5, the "acquiescence by B theorem." It reads as follows:

With full information conditions, assumption 2.A.7b, . . . and strict preferences, Acq_B is a full-information equilibrium outcome of the international interaction game if and only if the equilibrium outcome of the crisis subgame at node 5 is either Cap_B or War_A, and for State B, $Acq_B > War_A$. (p. 81)

---

96. For example, when testing whether or not the model successfully predicts "acquiescence by state B," Bueno de Mesquita and Lalman present a 2×2 table comparing observed and predicted outcomes. Entries on the main diagonal of this table (Yes/Yes or No/No) appear to be successful predictions, but the 442 entries in the No/No cell contain both cases where the model successfully predicted a specific outcome different from Acq_B (such as "capitulation") *and* cases where it predicted an outcome other than Acq_B but where some other outcome (different from both Acq_B and the predicted outcome) actually occurred. Collapsing categories in this way thus masks the unsuccessful predictions. See Bueno de Mesquita and Lalman, *War and Reason*, pp. 81–85; and Curtis S. Signorino, "Estimation and Strategic Interaction in Discrete Choice Models of International Conflict," Occasional Paper No. 98–4 (Cambridge, Mass.: Weatherhead Center for International Affairs, Harvard University, 1998), pp. 20–23.

97. Bueno de Mesquita has previously emphasized the problem of internal validity in large-N research, noting that "the close scrutiny of individual decisions yields better estimates of utilities than do gross applications of general evaluative criteria." See Bueno de Mesquita, "Toward a Scientific Understanding," p. 133.

As discussed earlier, the manner of presentation is not very transparent, and one must refer back to the original model and assumptions to figure out what is actually being said. Once translated, however, this proposition in effect predicts that state *B* will acquiesce to state *A*'s demands if it prefers acquiescing to beginning a war itself *or* to letting the opponent (state *A*) begin the war.

Bueno de Mesquita and Lalman illustrate this hypothesis with a brief case study of the 1898 Fashoda crisis between Great Britain and France. To do this properly, one would want to obtain independent evidence about British and French preferences, and then show that each side acted as the model predicts. Specifically, one would have to show that the leaders of each state held the preferences identified in Proposition 3.5, and that France backed down because it preferred that outcome to a war launched by Britain. Ideally, one would also seek evidence showing that the key elites made the choices they did via a process of reasoning at least roughly similar to the mechanism implied by the model. Yet the only evidence that Bueno de Mesquita and Lalman provide about French preferences is a quotation by French Foreign Minister Théophile Delcassé, stating that "war is preferable to national dishonor" (quoted on p. 84).

In short, the *model* says France will acquiesce only if it prefers this outcome to war, yet the French foreign minister apparently believed exactly the opposite. It is possible (even likely) that Delcassé was bluffing and his statement was not a true reflection of French preferences. Nonetheless, given that this is the only independent evidence Bueno de Mesquita and Lalman provide about French preferences, the case (as they portray it) actually contradicts their theoretical argument.

The Greco-Turkish Confrontation in Cyprus. A second example follows from their analysis of the democratic peace literature. To explain why democracies do not fight each other whereas democracies and nondemocracies do, Bueno de Mesquita and Lalman argue that democracies face higher domestic constraints to using force and that this is common knowledge. As a result, all democracies know that they prefer peace to war, and each knows that other democracies know this, so war between them is not a rational outcome.

When a democracy and a nondemocracy face each other, however, their model identifies two main paths to war. In the first path, the nondemocracy assumes that the democracy is reluctant to use force and attacks, mistakenly believing that the democracy will capitulate. In the second path, which is the one emphasized by Bueno de Mesquita and Lalman, the democracy fears that the nondemocracy will try to exploit its reluctance to use force and chooses to preempt, thereby obtaining the first-strike advantage. In their words, "The high domestic political constraint faced by democracies makes them vulnerable to threats of war or exploitation and liable to launch preemptive attacks against presumed aggressors" (p. 159). This result seems quite counterintuitive: for democracies, their reluctance to use force actually makes them more likely to employ it![98]

Unfortunately, this surprising result is not well supported by the empirical record, including the evidence contained in *War and Reason* itself. Bueno de Mesquita and Lalman suggest that democracies are prone to preempt in a crisis, but more extensive empirical studies have shown that preemptive wars are very rare and that democracies almost never fight preventive wars.[99] The outbreaks of World Wars I and II contradict their model as well, insofar as none of the threatened democracies tried to launch a preemptive attack on their nondemocratic adversaries. Furthermore, the model suggests that domestic constraints are the key to the democratic war puzzle, whereas other empirical studies have suggested that normative factors or alliance commitments are more important.[100]

Finally, and most important for our purposes, the evidence presented by Bueno de Mesquita and Lalman often undermines their own argument. First, as already discussed, the 1898 Fashoda crisis was a confrontation between two democracies, but the dovish nature of democracies and their ability to signal peaceful intentions played little or no role in its outcome (and is not even mentioned in their own account).[101] Second, to show how democracies and nondemocracies interact in ways that lead the former to use force preemptively, Bueno de Mesquita and Lalman offer a brief case study comparing the 1967 and 1974 confrontations between Greece and Turkey over Cyprus. In 1967 the use of force was averted, but democratic Turkey occupied the disputed

---

98. As they elaborate: "If the first-strike advantage is large enough, *A* will prefer to initiate the use of force rather than risk being compelled to capitulate or to fight under the most adverse conditions. Thus, *A's* democratic institutions make it susceptible to exploitation and incline it toward preemption." See Bueno de Mesquita and Lalman, *War and Reason,* pp. 159–160.

99. See Randall L. Schweller, "Domestic Structure and Preventive War: Are the Democratic States More Pacific?" *World Politics,* Vol. 44, No. 1 (January 1992), pp. 235–269; and Dan Reiter, "Exploding the Powder Keg Myth: Preemptive Wars Almost Never Happen," *International Security,* Vol. 20, No. 2 (Fall 1995), pp. 5–34.

100. See, in particular, Bruce Russett, *Grasping the Democratic Peace* (Princeton, N.J.: Princeton University Press, 1995), pp. 86–93, 119–120; and Joanne Gowa, *Ballots and Bullets* (Princeton, N.J.: Princeton University Press, forthcoming).

101. On Fashoda, see Christopher Layne, "Kant or Cant"; and Susan Peterson, "The Lessons of the Fashoda Crisis for Democratic Peace Theory," *Security Studies,* Vol. 5, No. 1 (Autumn 1995), pp. 3–37.

island in 1974. They argue that the absence of force in 1967 and its employment in 1974 are both consistent with their theoretical predictions.

Unfortunately, this case neither constitutes a rigorous test nor offers persuasive support for their argument. The model predicts that Turkey will preempt to prevent Greece from taking advantage of the domestic constraints on Turkey's use of force, yet they offer no evidence demonstrating that this is in fact the reason Turkey chose to act in 1974 but not in 1967. More important, this case is a poor choice for testing this proposition because the democratic Greek government was overthrown by a military coup at the beginning of the 1967 crisis. Thus Greece was not a democracy in either 1967 or 1974, yet Turkey did not use force in the first confrontation but did use force in the second. Faced with this clear challenge to the model, they argue that the Greek military dictatorship faced domestic constraints that were "more typical of a democracy" (p. 162). This sort of flexible coding is the antithesis of scholarly rigor, and casts further doubt on the empirical validity of the model.

The Sino-Indian Border War. Bueno de Mesquita and Lalman also include a case study of the Sino-Indian border war of 1962. Although this case is included to illustrate a proposition about the impact of shifts in the balance of power, their explanation for the war is the same as the causal mechanism they depict for a war between a democracy and a nondemocracy. In their words: "All the conditions for war were there. India believed China preferred to capitulate rather than fight back. China knew India held this belief. China sought negotiation and offered concessions, whereas India sought capitulation or acquiescence. The Chinese were prepared to fight back, but India, a low probability of success in war notwithstanding, pursued the use of force through its forward policy. China ultimately met force with force" (p. 202). This is precisely the causal pattern suggested for a preemptive war begun by a democracy against a nondemocratic challenger; the only problem is that the regime types are exactly the opposite of the ones depicted by the model! In this case, China (a nondemocracy) is acting the way that their model says a democracy should behave (i.e., it is reluctant to use force and prefers negotiation, but eventually preempts when pressed). India (a democracy) is acting the way the model says that authoritarian challengers will behave (i.e., it is trying to take advantage of the other side's reluctance to use force). Yet the contradiction is never explained.

Thus the three case studies they provide of democratic-democratic and democratic-nondemocratic interactions either do not support or actually contradict the predictions of the model. The empirical record is not being used to test the theory; it is being tailored to fit it.

In sum, neither the quantitative analysis nor the case studies contained in *War and Reason* provides compelling empirical support for the theoretical model developed in the book. Significantly, neither type of test is performed in an especially careful or rigorous fashion—among other things, the case studies themselves appear to be based on a cursory number of historical sources—and little effort is made to test the model directly. Although Bueno de Mesquita and Lalman are to be commended for stressing the importance of empirical testing, their effort does not achieve a high standard of scientific rigor.

EXAMPLE NO. 11. Emerson M.S. Niou, Peter C. Ordeshook, and Gregory F. Rose, *The Balance of Power: Stability in International Systems*.[102] This book is an ambitious effort to formalize balance-of-power theory, and to test the resulting model through an in-depth study of great power diplomacy. Unlike most of the recent formal work on security topics, which uses two-person, noncooperative game theory, *The Balance of Power* relies on *n*-person, cooperative game theory.[103] Although in many ways an exemplary study (the presentation is reasonably clear and accessible, and the authors frequently acknowledge the limits of their model), the empirical results are not convincing.

The central focus of the book is the concept of *stability*, which takes two forms. System stability refers to any distribution of resources in which none of the "essential" members can be eliminated by the others. Resource stability, by contrast, refers to situations where there is no incentive or capacity to alter the existing distribution of resources. The central question, therefore, is under what conditions will a given international system exhibit either form of stability.[104]

To answer this question, Niou, Ordeshook, and Rose construct an *n*-person model of the international system. The model assumes that states seek to maximize their share of the system's resources while preserving their own independence. It further assumes that (1) all states have perfect information, (2) resources are infinitely divisible and readily transferable, (3) states prefer to gain additional resources through negotiation rather than war, and (4) all

---

102. Emerson M.S. Niou, Peter C. Ordeshook, and Gregory F. Rose, *The Balance of Power: Stability in International Systems* (Cambridge, U.K.: Cambridge University Press, 1989).

103. In cooperative game theory, players can communicate and make binding agreements; in noncooperative game theory, binding agreements are forbidden and communication may or may not be permitted. A central question for cooperative game theory is what types of coalitions are likely to form among the players, as each seeks an arrangement that will maximize their own utility.

104. A system that is "resource stable" is also "system stable" (after all, eliminating an essential actor would by definition alter the distribution of resources), but it may be possible to alter the distribution of resources without eliminating an essential member.

states grow at an equal rate.[105] The model yields a healthy number of unsurprising results as well as a number of more interesting and counterintuitive predictions. In particular, Niou, Ordeshook, and Rose demonstrate that system and resource stability can be achieved simultaneously only when one state controls exactly 50 percent of the resources in the system.

The basic logic is straightforward: when one state has exactly 50 percent of the resources in the system, the others must cooperate with one another and isolate it, because any further increase in the strongest state's resources would allow it to absorb the others. Paradoxically, this result implies that any state (or coalition) that is facing the threat of elimination can avoid it by voluntarily transferring resources to the strongest state until the other state controls exactly 50 percent. Because all states know that this tactic is possible, certain distributions of power may be resource stable if all members realize that they could not unilaterally improve their share of resources (taking into account how the other members will respond). The model also implies that wars will never occur, because rational states would prefer to readjust resources through negotiation and voluntary transfers rather than through the use of force.

Niou, Ordeshook, and Rose test the model through an empirical analysis of European great power diplomacy in the period 1870–1914. In contrast to the statistical procedures used in *War and Reason,* their statistical procedures are explicated clearly and are generally convincing, and the historical narrative is based on an array of primary and secondary sources.[106] What is lacking, unfortunately, is a strong correspondence between the theoretical model and the empirical results.[107]

First, the bulk of the empirical testing involves a comparison of the gains from different alliance combinations, measured by an index of material capabilities. The authors predict that states will prefer coalitions that are just large enough to win (meaning they are larger than any combination of the remaining actors), while maximizing their own share of the overall alliance resources.[108]

---

105. Some of these assumptions are subsequently relaxed in order to analyze specific issues. In chapter 5, for example, they relax the assumption of equal growth in order to investigate the logic of preventive war.
106. In terms of pages, more than 25 percent of *The Balance of Power* is devoted to a discussion of measurement procedures, empirical tests, and historical narratives.
107. For a judicious but telling critique of the Niou, Ordeshook, and Rose results, see Snyder, "Alliances, Balance, and Stability."
108. Formally, they show that if $g(c)$ equals a state's gains from alliance C and $r(c)$ equals the total resources in C (i.e., the sum of each member's capabilities), then states in the system will choose allies in order to maximize $g(c)/r(c)$. They do not necessarily assume proportionality, however,

They present a series of tables summarizing the gains from different alliance combinations, and some of the results are clearly consistent with the model. Unfortunately, these results depend on a series of ad hoc restrictions that are wholly separate from the earlier theoretical analyses, and alliances that do not fit are explained by invoking other exogenous factors. Thus they arbitrarily exclude the possibility of a Franco-German alliance because of the conflict over Alsace-Lorraine, and they invoke German "mistrust" of Russia to explain why Germany chose a less profitable alliance with Austria. Similarly, Britain is excluded in some cases because its interests conflicted with several potential partners, even when the model predicts that these coalitions would have brought it greater resources. Instead of vindicating the formal model, in short, the empirical analysis ultimately relies on ad hoc factors like interest, revisionism, or ideology.

Second, the central mechanism contained in the model—the voluntary transfer of resources from declining state(s) to strong states (up to the level of 50 percent of total resources)—is largely absent from the empirical discussion. And when it does appear, the authors recognize that this mechanism is not a realistic possibility. Thus, although they mention that France and Germany might have been brought together by a German decision to relinquish Alsace-Lorraine, they add that this step "would almost certainly have led to the demise of the nascent German state" (p. 262). The absence of such transfers from the empirical account is not surprising, of course. Real states in the real world are notoriously reluctant to transfer resources (voluntarily) to more powerful rivals, and certainly not on the scale that is implied in the model.[109]

More generally, although the narrative in the empirical chapters is couched in formal terms, there is little direct evidence showing that policymakers made choices for the reasons depicted in the model. Such evidence may not be entirely necessary to prove the worth of a formal explanation, but a rigorous effort to test the theory would have sought at least some evidence indicating that states made alliance choices or war decisions in roughly the manner they imply. Instead of using history to test the model, in short, the model is used to organize the historical narrative.

---

which means that a state might in some circumstances receive gains larger than its initial contribution to the coalition. See Niou, Ordeshook, and Rose, *Balance of Power*, p. 220.
109. It is also worth noting that territorial cessions have been declining steadily over the past two centuries, probably as a consequence of the rise of nationalism and political participation in most great powers.

Finally, the historical analysis of World War I is unconvincing. Because the model views war as inherently irrational, the outbreak of fighting in July 1914 can be explained only by domestic politics, misperception, asymmetrical growth, or some other exogenous factor. Using the model and their statistical analysis as a guide, Niou, Ordeshook, and Rose reject the view that World War I was caused by German fears of rising Russian power. Instead, they argue that it was in effect a preventive war begun by Russia, intended to check the rise of German power. As Germany approached preponderance, the model says that it would be countered by a coalition of the rest. But because this response was not possible (for various exogenous reasons), they argue that Russia was forced to choose the second-best alternative of preventive war. Yet they offer no evidence that key Russian elites saw the July crisis as an opportunity for preventive war; on the contrary, there is abundant historical evidence that Germany was the driving force throughout the crisis. At best, the analysis of World War I is not a rigorous test of the model; at worst, it underscores its limitations.[110]

In sum, although the model is logically consistent and the authors make an admirable attempt to demonstrate its empirical value, *The Balance of Power* is not a persuasive demonstration of the power of formal theory. Formalization does not clarify the argument and does not lead to new, well-confirmed hypotheses, and the empirical evidence does not support the main theoretical claims. Although the authors deserve praise for their ambitious effort to combine rigorous formal analysis with careful historical research, the results cast additional doubt on the claim that formal theory is an intrinsically superior approach to the study of international politics in general and security affairs in particular.

Conclusion

Several conclusions may be drawn from this survey of formal rational choice approaches to security studies. First, formal theory is most useful for enhancing the precision of a theory, and for verifying and refining its deductive logic.

---

110. In contrast to their behavior in the 1909 Bosnian crisis, German officials repeatedly pressed Austria to inflict harsh measures on Serbia in 1914. Key German officials were also obsessed with the specter of rising Russian power and the growing cohesion of the Triple Entente. As Chancellor Theobald von Bethmann Hollweg put it in 1909, "The future belongs to Russia, as it grows and weighs upon us like an ever-deepening nightmare." See David G. Hermann, *The Arming of Europe and the Making of the First World War* (Princeton, N.J.: Princeton University Press, 1996), p. 214.

This can be a valuable contribution, and provides ample justification for the continued use of formal techniques.

Second, formalization has not led to powerful new explanations of important real-world phenomena. For the most part, recent formal work has tended to take arguments derived from other scholars and place them in mathematical form. Such efforts have helped qualify and refine these existing theories, but the initial creative insights have generally come from scholars employing other approaches.

Third, recent formal work generally lacks rigorous empirical support. Formal theorists have devoted relatively little effort to testing their propositions, and the tests they have provided are often unconvincing. Although there are good reasons to value formal theory, in short, it should not be seen as inherently more valuable or "scientific" than other well-established research traditions.

Taken together, these characteristics help explain why recent formal work has had relatively little to say about important real-world security issues. Although formal techniques produce precise, logically consistent arguments, they often rest on unrealistic assumptions and the results are rarely translated into clear and accessible conclusions. And because many formal conjectures are often untested, policymakers and concerned citizens have no way of knowing if the arguments are valid.

In this sense, much of the recent formal work in security studies reflects the "cult of irrelevance" that pervades much of contemporary social science. Instead of using their expertise to address important real-world problems, academics often focus on narrow and trivial problems that may impress their colleagues but are of little practical value. If formal theory were to dominate security studies as it has other areas of political science, much of the scholarship in the field would likely be produced by people with impressive technical skills but little or no substantive knowledge of history, politics, or strategy.[111] Such fields are prone to become "method-driven" rather than "problem-driven," as research topics are chosen not because they are important but

---

111. The field of economics offers a cautionary tale. A 1990 survey of elite economics graduate programs reported that 68 percent of the students believed a "thorough knowledge of the economy" was unimportant for professional success; indeed, only 3.4 percent thought such knowledge was "very important." Similarly, the American Economic Association's commission on graduate education warned in 1988 of "the extent to which graduate education in economics may have become too removed from real economic problems. . . . graduate programs may be turning out a generation with too many *idiots savants*, skilled in technique but innocent of real economic issues." See Arjo Klamer and David Colander, *The Making of Economists* (Boulder, Colo.: Westview, 1990), p. 18; and Mayer, *Truth versus Precision in Economics*, p. 159.

because they are amenable to analysis by the reigning *méthode du jour*.[112] Instead of being a source of independent criticism and creative, socially useful ideas, the academic world becomes an isolated community engaged solely in dialogue with itself.[113]

Throughout most of the postwar period, the field of security studies managed to avoid this danger. It has been theoretically and methodologically diverse, but its agenda has been shaped more by real-world problems than by methodological fads. New theoretical or methodological innovations have been brought to bear on particular research puzzles, but the field as a whole has retained considerable real-world relevance.

By contrast, recent formal work in security studies has little to say about contemporary security issues. Formal rational choice theorists have been largely absent from the major international security debates of the past decade (such as the nature of the post–Cold War world; the character, causes, and strength of the democratic peace; the potential contribution of security institutions; the causes of ethnic conflict; the future role of nuclear weapons; or the impact of ideas and culture on strategy and conflict). These debates have been launched and driven primarily by scholars using nonformal methods, and formal theorists have joined in only after the central parameters were established by others.[114] Thus one of the main strengths of the subfield of security studies—namely, its close connection to real-world issues—could be lost if the narrow tendencies of the modeling community took control of its research agenda.

The solution should be obvious, however. Instead of embracing formal rational choice theory as the only true way to do science or seeking to banish

---

112. Even the mathematical economist Gerard Debreu, in a speech extolling the virtues of formalization, has warned that "the values imprinted on an economist by his study of mathematics . . . do not play a silent role: they may play a decisive role. The very choice of the question to which [a mathematical economist] tries to find answers is influenced by his mathematical background. *Thus the danger is ever present that the part of economics will become secondary, if not marginal to that judgement."* See Debreu, "Mathematization of Economic Theory," pp. 4–5 (emphasis added).
113. For a practitioner's views, see David Newsom, "Foreign Policy and Academia," *Foreign Policy,* No. 101 (Winter 1995–96), pp. 52–67.
114. An interesting example of this tendency is Rui J.P. de Figueiredo, Jr., and Barry R. Weingast, "The Rationality of Fear: Political Opportunism and Ethnic Conflict," in Barbara F. Walter and Jack L. Snyder, eds., *Civil War, Insecurity, and Intervention* (New York: Columbia University Press, 1999), which formalizes several earlier writings on the origins of ethnic conflict. Their model implies that ethnic conflict is more likely when (1) endangered elites "gamble for resurrection" by stirring up ethnic hatred, (2) when the opposing groups act in ways that appear to confirm the elites' claims that they are a threat, and (3) when the perceived cost of failing to heed these warnings is high. In other words, ethnic conflict is more likely when one ethnic group has reason to believe that the another group is hostile and that ignoring the potential threat might be fatal.

it from the field, members of the security studies profession should actively strive to retain the intellectual and methodological diversity of our field. Just as natural sciences profit from the fruitful collaboration of theoreticians and experimentalists, security studies should welcome contributions from formal theory, large-N statistical analysis, historical case studies, and even the more rigorous forms of interpretive or constructivist analysis.[115] Although individual scholars will emphasize different techniques in their own work and place different values on the contributions made by each approach, the field as a whole will be far richer if such diversity is retained *and esteemed*.[116] Given the continued relevance of security issues and the tragic consequences that accompany ignorance, it would be irresponsible to accept anything less.

---

115. Hacking once again provides the appropriate caution: "What is scientific method? Is it the experimental method? The question is wrongly posed. Why should there be *the* method of science? There is not just one way to build a house, or even to grow tomatoes. We should not expect something as motley as the growth of knowledge to be strapped to one methodology." See Hacking, *Representing and Intervening*, p. 152.

116. As Peter C. Ordeshook has observed, "Regardless of the mathematical rigor of our models, we need to drop the view of science as an enterprise directed by academics armed with theorems and lemmas or by experimentalists scurrying about in white smocks. Science proceeds less coherently, through induction and deduction informed by attempts to be practical and to manipulate real things, where those manipulations rely as much on experience, intuition, and creative insight as on theory." See Ordeshook, "Engineering or Science: What Is the Study of Politics?" in *Critical Review,* Vol. 9, Nos. 1–2 (Winter–Spring 1995), p. 180. See also the defense of methodological pluralism offered by Gabriel A. Almond in "Separate Tables: Schools and Sects in Political Science," *PS: Political Science and Politics,* Vol. 23, No. 4 (Fall 1988), pp. 828–842.

Sorting Through the Wealth of Notions

Bruce Bueno de Mesquita and James D. Morrow

The opportunity to better inform the readership of *International Security* on the important contributions of a rational choice perspective is most welcome. We and Stephen Walt agree on many issues. He says that "[social science] requires theories that are . . . logically consistent,"[1] and that "formal techniques facilitate the construction of precise and deductively sound arguments" (p. 8). Walt asserts, correctly we believe, that "the formal language of mathematics can impart greater precision to an argument, and helps guard against inconsistencies arising either from a failure to spell out the causal logic in detail or from ambiguities of normal language" (p. 14) and that the "virtues [of formal theory] should not be dismissed lightly" (p. 15). We agree completely with these views.

Walt raises issues worthy of fuller discussion. He contends, and we agree, that "the central aim of social science is to develop knowledge that is relevant to understanding important social problems. Among other things, this task requires theories that are precise, logically consistent, original, and empirically valid" (p. 8). We discuss how the rational choice approach to security studies contributes significantly in these ways. Additionally, we address some misrepresentations in Walt's article.

The Centrality of Logical Consistency for Scientific Theories

Walt gives three criteria for evaluating social science theories: logical consistency, degree of originality, and empirical validity. We believe that logical consistency takes precedence over the other two criteria; without logical consistency, neither the originality of a theory nor its empirical validity can be judged. Logical consistency is the first test of a theory because consistency is necessary, though not sufficient, for understanding how international politics works.

Bruce Bueno de Mesquita is Senior Fellow at the Hoover Institution, Stanford University. He is finishing a textbook, Principles of International Politics, *to be published by Congressional Quarterly Press later this year. James D. Morrow is Senior Research Fellow at the Hoover Institution, Stanford University.*

We thank Robert Powell and Frank Zagare for their comments on an earlier draft.

1. Stephen M. Walt, "Rigor or Rigor Mortis? Rational Choice and Security Studies," *International Security*, Vol. 23, No. 4 (Spring 1999), pp. 5–48, at p. 8. Subsequent references to Walt's article appear in the text.

International Security, Vol. 24, No. 2 (Fall 1999), pp. 56–73

A basic point in logic drives our view. A theory, in terms of logic, consists of a system of assumptions and conclusions derived from those assumptions. A logical inconsistency exists when two mutually contradictory statements can be derived from the assumptions of a theory. When such a contradiction exists in a theory, then *any statement* follows logically from the theory. There is, then, no discipline for arguments in a logically inconsistent theory; those using the theory are free to draw any conclusion they wish from the premises of the theory.

Logical inconsistencies deny the possibility of a theory having empirical content. Theories derive empirical content by producing falsifiable hypotheses, conclusions that could be contradicted by evidence. A theory gains credence as more of its falsifiable propositions are supported by evidence, although there are no hard and fast rules here. However, because *any* pattern of evidence can be matched with some conclusion of a logically inconsistent theory, such theories cannot be falsified and so cannot have empirical content. A theory is falsified when an alternative is shown to fit the range of predictions better than the initial theory. Falsification of a theory cannot happen if any evidence can be interpreted as an implication of the theory.

Theories with logical inconsistencies can also appear highly original simply because there are no constraints on reaching conclusions. Such a theory appears to "explain" all previous results while also allowing its proposer to advance any claims that appear to reflect the historical record as she sees it. The originality of a logically inconsistent theory is dubious at best.

Further, logically inconsistent theories present serious problems for policy prescriptions, a central goal of social science theory according to Walt. Again, any conclusion can be derived when a logical inconsistency exists, and so the choice of which conclusion to use for policy purposes falls entirely on the tastes or prejudices of the party making the prescription. Indeed, the use of a logically inconsistent theory to justify a policy recommendation is worse than recommendations not supported by any theory. Policy recommendations based on an inconsistent theory use the appearance of social science to cover their lack of supporting argument and evidence.

For these reasons, we believe that logical consistency has pride of place among the criteria for judging social science theories. Other criteria, particularly empirical content, are also critical. We do not believe that it is sufficient for social science merely to pass a test of logical consistency. Rather, logical inconsistencies undermine all other criteria, and so take precedence over those other criteria.

SOME PRACTICAL MATTERS IN THE DEVELOPMENT OF THEORY

It is rarely the case that theories with well-known logical inconsistencies persist in any field, although vague or incomplete theories do. The practical problems in the development of scientific theories lie in unexposed inconsistencies in arguments. Few theories are sufficiently elaborated that the complete logic is known and all the conclusions tested against evidence. Research strives to improve knowledge by refining or inventing theories that fit the empirical record better and that remedy logical problems.

Walt is correct when he quotes Larry Laudan that "'inconsistent theories have often been detected in almost all . . . branches of science,' and argues that efforts to resolve such inconsistencies often form an important part of specific research traditions" (p. 16) and that "the only conceivable response to a conceptual problem of this kind is to refuse to accept the offending theory until the inconsistency is corrected" (p. 16 n. 29).[2] That is, the resolution of logical inconsistencies through the exploration of the logic of a theory is a central part of the scientific enterprise.

This is why the two of us use formal models in our research. We find that the discipline of formal models forces us to confront logical inconsistencies in the theories we study. Of course, formalism is not necessary for the analysis of the logic of a theory. The rigor of mathematics, however, does force the analyst using formal methods to confront logical problems that can be missed in purely verbal arguments.

What logical problems are likely to arise in the development of a theory? First, assumptions necessary for the argument may be unstated. Because verbal arguments often rely on the eloquence of their presentation rather than the logic of their argument, the author may leave out critical assumptions. Indeed, the author may be unaware of the omission of a necessary assumption. Many of Walt's examples of logically inconsistent and yet fruitful theories are really examples of logically incomplete or vague theories. Certainly, parts of Kenneth Waltz's neorealist theory fall into this category.[3] Formal models, however, require a fuller statement of assumptions, and so force the author to come to

2. Larry Laudan, *Progress and Its Problems: Towards a Theory of Scientific Growth* (Berkeley: University of California Press, 1977), pp. 49–50.
3. Kenneth N. Waltz, *Theory of International Politics* (Reading, Mass.: Addison-Wesley, 1979). Waltz's theory also illustrates the difficulties created by inconsistency. On p. 109 he argues that "states face a prisoners' dilemma." Yet Waltz also says that "politics among the European great powers tended toward the model of a zero-sum game. Each power viewed another's loss as its own gain" (p. 70). The prisoners' dilemma is not zero-sum and, in repeated play, it has cooperative equilibria. Two-player zero-sum games never have cooperative equilibria. How are we to interpret a theory that says international politics are both zero-sum and not? This inconsistency may lead different neorealists to arrive at opposite conclusions about the prospects of cooperation among states. See

terms with the assumptions of the argument and allow the reader to view them in their totality.[4] When such assumptions are visible to the reader in their complete form, the reader can take exception to them, replace them with alternate assumptions, and then pursue the modified argument to its logical conclusions. Establishing the unstated assumptions of a theory is one common example of scientific progress through logical elaboration.

A second problem is that a theory may appear to lead to contradictory conclusions when it does not because the relevant contingencies have not been specified. Close logical analysis, as done in formal models, can solve this problem by identifying the lacuna in the flawed argument. A revised version of the theory may show how one of the conclusions holds under certain, previously unspecified conditions, while the apparent contradiction holds in others.

Third, logical analysis can show that seemingly disparate, known empirical regularities actually follow from a single theory. That is, logical analysis can unify accepted results within one theory, and so improve our knowledge by creating connections that did not exist before. Unifying known results within one theory is scientific progress even though it provides no new empirical discoveries.

Formal models are not necessary for any of these improvements in the logic of a theory; we and others find them helpful. Close logical analysis is demanding, and formal models require logical rigor. The game-theoretic models we use force us to be clear in our assumptions about who the actors are, the choices they face, the consequences of those choices, how the actors evaluate the possible outcomes, and what information each has at each choice. All of this can be done in a verbal argument, but such specificity is rarely seen outside of formal models.

Commonly accepted theories or known empirical regularities are one fertile ground for the application of formal models, as is the development of novel ideas. Are existing theories logically sound, and if not, how can their logical

---

Charles L. Glaser, "Realists as Optimists: Cooperation as Self-Help," *International Security*, Vol. 19, No. 3 (Winter 1994/95), pp. 50–90; and John J. Mearsheimer, "The False Promise of International Institutions," ibid., pp. 5–49. Even James D. Morrow's typographical error on p. 89 of his *Game Theory for Political Scientists* (Princeton, N.J.: Princeton University Press, 1994) cannot make the prisoners' dilemma a zero-sum game!

4. A personal example makes this point. Bruce Bueno de Mesquita, James D. Morrow, and Ethan Zorick claim the existence of a surprising equilibrium in a crisis bargaining game in "Capabilities, Perception, and Escalation," *American Political Science Review*, Vol. 91, No. 1 (March 1997), pp. 15–27. The "equilibrium" is the product of a mathematical error. Because all assumptions are explicit, the error was discovered. There is no debate, and a correction will be published. In formal models, the logic is reproducible so that errors are readily discovered.

inconsistencies be removed? How do those logical remedies change the conclusions of the theory, and so its empirical predictions? Rather than striking out only for novel arguments in every paper, we and others also examine well-established theories to test and refine their logic. Not surprisingly, those models often produce well-known conclusions. Sometimes, they produce surprising results. A claim that such models contribute nothing requires more than just a recitation of the well-known conclusions that follow from the model. These efforts contribute by showing which "well-known" conclusions do not follow from the model, as suggested in the earlier quotation from Laudan, thereby sorting out a confusion of hypotheses that might contradict one another. Models that try to capture well-known theories also contribute by connecting previously unconnected empirical results in a unified explanation. Further, such models provide a baseline for future developments that depart from existing arguments in novel directions. In that way, the original model allows us to judge the impact of changes in the assumptions of the theory.

The question of judging theories is separate from originality as measured by the source of scientific inspiration. Scientists have drawn inspiration from any number of sources, including mystic beliefs, for hypotheses that later proved to be true. Walt's article sometimes confounds the source of scientific inspiration with the criteria for judging the results of that inspiration (pp. 30–31, 47). We think it does not matter from where scientists draw their hypotheses, provided that the hypotheses are subjected to logical examination and rigorous empirical testing.

All of the criteria for judging scientific theories are guides to improving knowledge because few theories are complete and final. We, like Walt, do not think that theories that contain logical inconsistencies should be abandoned solely on those grounds; instead, their errors should be remedied. In the sections that remain, we show how the formal literature promotes logical consistency and the consequences of that for fostering scientific progress.

Rigor and Insight: What Does the Formal Literature Say?

Walt surveys several papers that use formal models to study questions in international politics and argues that the formal literature lacks creativity and empirical tests. One article cannot survey an entire literature. In this section, we briefly discuss some papers Walt mentions and others that he does not to help the reader gain a clearer image of the recent literature that uses models to study international politics. The discussion first provides examples in which rational choice models (1) clarify unstated assumptions in prior research;

(2) eliminate apparent contradictions by identifying the contingencies underlying cases; (3) tie known empirical regularities together in a unified logical
framework; and (4) identify previously accepted results that do not follow. We
go on to discuss novel results in the formal literature not mentioned by Walt
and close this section with a sampling of inaccuracies in Walt's charac-
terizations of specific publications.

Robert Powell shows that Thomas Schelling's argument about the reciprocal
fear of surprise attack depends on an unstated assumption.[5] Powell demonstrates that the reciprocal fear of surprise attack requires the assumption that
states in a nuclear crisis do not have the option to end the crisis by surrendering the stakes. Unrecognized by Schelling and a massive informal literature, if
either has the option to end the crisis by surrendering the stakes, nuclear war
cannot occur except by accident.

James Morrow's study of asymmetric alliances identifies contingent circumstances under which states form alliances for reasons other than security.[6] He
shows that many alliances are asymmetric in their aims, with one side gaining
security at the expense of some of its autonomy and the other side acquiring
greater freedom of action at the expense of a heightened risk of being entan-
gled in its partner's disputes. This study makes clear why the prevalent view
of alliances cannot apply in all cases and provides a novel logic that accounts
both for the many cases that do not fit the standard view and for those that do.

Bruce Bueno de Mesquita, Morrow, Randolph Siverson, and Alastair Smith
construct a model to investigate the logical foundations for the observed
regularities associated with the democratic peace, demonstrating how formal
models can unify seemingly unrelated facts.[7] They show that a simple model
accounts for diverse observations, including: (1) democracies tend not to fight
wars with one another; (2) democracies fight nondemocracies with regularity;
(3) democracies win a disproportionate share of the wars they fight; (4) democracies are more inclined to resolve disputes through negotiation or mediation
than are autocracies; (5) all else being equal, democracies are more likely to
initiate war against autocracies than are autocracies to initiate war against

5. Robert Powell, "Crisis Stability in the Nuclear Age," *American Political Science Review*, Vol. 83,
No. 1 (March 1989), pp. 61–76; Powell, *Nuclear Deterrence Theory: The Search for Credibility* (New
York: Cambridge University Press, 1990); and Thomas C. Schelling, *Arms and Influence* (New
Haven, Conn.: Yale University Press, 1966).
6. James D. Morrow, "Alliances and Asymmetry: An Alternative to the Capability Aggregation
Model of Alliances," *American Journal of Political Science*, Vol. 35, No. 4 (November 1991), pp. 904–
933.
7. Bruce Bueno de Mesquita, James D. Morrow, Randolph M. Siverson, and Alastair Smith, "An
Institutional Explanation of the Democratic Peace," *American Political Science Review*, Vol. 93, No.
4 (forthcoming, December 1999).

democracies; (6) democracies are particularly likely to coerce into submission much smaller adversaries, including democratic rivals; and (7) democracies, when in a war, tend to suffer fewer casualties and tend to fight shorter wars than nondemocracies. The same theory, in other papers, accounts for significant variation in economic growth, human capital, war aims, and political survival rates of leaders.[8]

A commonly held view in international relations is that foreign policy decisionmaking improves when leaders seek advice from people holding diverse opinions.[9] Randall Calvert shows, to the contrary, that it is rational for political leaders to surround themselves with "yes-men," and that doing so enhances rather than harms effective policy.[10] Decisionmakers consider the source of opinions on policy and discount for the biases of those sources. When a leader receives a contrary opinion from a frequent critic, the leader is likely to credit that judgment to the bias of the critic. When a leader receives advice against her policy from an adviser whose views usually are the same as hers, she is likely to reassess her judgment. This adviser's disagreement cannot be attributed to a general bias against the leader's viewpoint.

A Fuller Picture

Walt's review article could not possibly discuss all of the research within the formal modeling literature. To clarify additional contributions of this literature, we now summarize results from several papers Walt does not mention. Like Walt, we cannot possibly discuss all of the fine research given the limited space provided to us. What follows should be read as a sampler.

Woosang Kim and Morrow examine the consequences of long-term shifts in power on the likelihood of war.[11] Contrary to most treatments of this topic,

---

8. On war aims, see Bruce Bueno de Mesquita, James D. Morrow, Randolph M. Siverson, and Alastair Smith, "Inside Out: A Theory of Domestic Political Institutions and the Issues of International Conflict," Hoover Working Papers in International Relations (Stanford, Calif.: Hoover Institution, 1998). On economic growth and related matters, see Bueno de Mesquita, Morrow, Siverson, and Smith, "Policy Failure and Political Survival: The Contribution of Political Institutions," *Journal of Conflict Resolution*, Vol. 43, No. 2 (April 1999), pp. 147–161; and Bueno de Mesquita, Morrow, Siverson, and Smith, "Political Institutions, Political Survival, and Policy Success," in Bueno de Mesquita and Hilton Root, eds., *Governing for Prosperity* (New Haven, Conn.: Yale University Press, 2000).

9. See Alexander L. George, *Presidential Decisionmaking in Foreign Policy: The Effective Use of Information and Advice* (Boulder, Colo.: Westview, 1980).

10. Randall L. Calvert, "The Value of Biased Information," *Journal of Politics*, Vol. 47, No. 2 (May 1985), pp. 530–555.

11. Woosang Kim and James D. Morrow, "When Do Power Shifts Lead to War?" *American Journal of Political Science*, Vol. 36, No. 4 (November 1992), pp. 896–922. See also Morrow, "The Logic of

they demonstrate that war is more likely if the declining state is risk averse and the challenging state is risk acceptant.[12] Further, the period of transition when power is approximately equal between rivals is not particularly dangerous. Additionally, the rates of growth in power are irrelevant to the likelihood of war. All these hypotheses are tested against the evidence and are supported. The latter two and the conjunction of the three are novel.

Kenneth Schultz's formalization of domestic political debate provides a new way to think about the nexus between domestic politics and foreign policy.[13] Whereas it is commonplace to argue that partisanship should end at the water's edge, Schultz shows formally and demonstrates empirically that partisan debate disciplines democratic leaders to seek effective foreign policies, whereas nonpartisanship in foreign affairs invites foreign adventurism and potential disaster.

Morrow shows that U.S. presidents were more likely to offer significant concessions to the Soviet Union in arms control negotiations when domestic economic factors threatened their re-election prospects.[14] He also shows systematic effects of congressional action on arms control negotiations through legislation on defense. Morrow tests the propositions of his model and finds support. His argument challenges structural views of arms control by showing how domestic political considerations shape negotiations.

Joanne Gowa models how security externalities influence trade policy. She argues that security concerns make states reluctant to trade with prospective adversaries. Bipolar systems mitigate this problem by reducing uncertainty about who prospective rivals are.[15] Gowa and Edward Mansfield report supporting evidence for this deduction.[16] Subsequent formal research draws attention to the limited circumstances under which this effect is expected to

---

Overtaking," in Jacek Kugler and Douglas Lemke, eds., *Parity and War* (Ann Arbor: University of Michigan Press, 1996), pp. 313–330. For an alternative model of power shifts, see Robert Powell, "Uncertainty, Shifting Power, and Appeasement," *American Political Science Review*, Vol. 90, No. 4 (December 1996), pp. 749–764.

12. A.F.K. Organski, *World Politics* (New York: Alfred Knopf, 1958); Organski and Jacek Kugler, *The War Ledger* (Chicago: University of Chicago Press, 1980); and Robert Gilpin, *War and Change in World Politics* (New York: Cambridge University Press, 1981).

13. Kenneth A. Schultz, "Domestic Opposition and Signaling in International Crises," *American Political Science Review*, Vol. 92, No. 4 (December 1998), pp. 829–844.

14. James D. Morrow, "Electoral and Congressional Incentives and Arms Control," *Journal of Conflict Resolution*, Vol. 35, No. 2 (June 1991), pp. 243–263.

15. Joanne Gowa, "Bipolarity, Multipolarity, and Free Trade," *American Political Science Review*, Vol. 83, No. 4 (December 1989), pp. 1245–1256; and Gowa, *Allies, Adversaries, and International Trade* (Princeton, N.J.: Princeton University Press, 1994).

16. Joanne Gowa and Edward D. Mansfield, "Power Politics and International Trade," *American Political Science Review*, Vol. 87, No. 2 (June 1993), pp. 408–420.

hold.[17] The formal nature of Gowa's argument facilitated this theoretically fruitful debate.

George Downs and David Rocke model decisions by leaders facing disastrous military defeat.[18] Whereas it is commonplace to think that it is irrational for *states* to continue to fight when their defeat is imminent and continued fighting is costly, Downs and Rocke show that it is rational for *leaders* to take high risks in such situations. The downside risk for the leader is low and the upside for political resurrection is great. Their model provides a coherent explanation for the seemingly irrational acts of desperation common among leaders facing military defeat. They note that independently derived evidence supports their resurrection hypothesis.[19]

Alastair Smith addresses the puzzle of the reliability of alliances.[20] The dismal record of allies in coming to the defense of their partners leads many to infer that alliances are unreliable.[21] Smith shows formally that selection effects lead would-be aggressors to attack in exactly those cases when the allies are not expected to aid one another. He demonstrates in theory and shows empirically that the cases in which attacks are deterred involve allies who had significantly higher *expected* reliability than in those cases in which an attack did take place. He provides a theory that solves the puzzle of the dog that barks and the dog that does not.

Powell shows that a long shadow of the future can, as argued by Michael Taylor and Robert Axelrod, foster cooperation, but he also shows when a long shadow of the future fosters conflict.[22] A longer shadow of the future increases the benefits of the peaceful period that follows a military victory, increasing the benefits of victory and therefore the willingness to fight.

---

17. James D. Morrow, "When Do 'Relative Gains' Impede Trade?" *Journal of Conflict Resolution*, Vol. 21, No. 1 (February 1997), pp. 12–37.
18. George W. Downs and David M. Rocke, "Conflict, Agency, and Gambling for Resurrection," *American Journal of Political Science*, Vol. 38, No. 2 (May 1994), pp. 362–380.
19. Bruce Bueno de Mesquita and Randolph M. Siverson, "War and the Survival of Political Leaders," *American Political Science Review*, Vol. 89, No. 4 (December 1995), pp. 841–855; and Bueno de Mesquita, Siverson, and Gary Woller, "War and the Fate of Regimes," *American Political Science Review*, Vol. 86, No. 3 (September 1992), pp. 638–646.
20. Alastair Smith, "Alliance Formation and War," *International Studies Quarterly*, Vol. 39, No. 4 (December 1995), pp. 405–425.
21. Alan N. Sabrosky, "Interstate Alliances: Their Reliability and the Expansion of War," in J. David Singer, ed., *The Correlates of War II* (New York: Free Press, 1980); and John A. Vasquez, "The Steps to War: Toward a Scientific Explanation of Correlates of War Findings," *World Politics*, Vol. 40, No. 1 (October 1987), p. 119.
22. Robert Powell, "Guns, Butter, and Anarchy," *American Political Science Review*, Vol. 87, No. 1 (March 1993), p. 120; Michael Taylor, *Anarchy and Cooperation* (New York: John Wiley and Sons, 1976); and Robert Axelrod, *The Evolution of Cooperation* (New York: Basic Books, 1984).

We hope this sampler will tempt some readers to take a closer look at the formal, rational choice literature dealing with security studies. A place to begin is with informed reviews of this literature.[23]

ERRORS IN WALT'S CARICATURES

As we have noted, models often attempt to capture existing theories and such models, not surprisingly, reproduce some conclusions that are already known. Then it is easy to point to any number of "well-known" conclusions and claim that the literature lacks originality. The proper test of originality is whether these models produce novel results. Here we reexamine some of the papers that Walt discusses to show novel conclusions he ignores. (We refer to Walt's examples by using the numbers he gives to each of the example papers he cites.)

EXAMPLE NO. 1. James D. Morrow, "Capabilities, Uncertainty, and Resolve."[24] In addition to the conclusions that Walt mentions (p. 23), this paper also presents the first analysis of selection effects on unobservable resolve using a formal model. This paper is a precursor to James Fearon's discussion of selection effects, which Walt (p. 15) describes as an important contribution of the formal theory literature.

EXAMPLE NO. 4. David Lalman and David Newman, "Alliance Formation and National Security."[25] Walt describes their conclusion that "nations *generally* enter into alliances in the expectation of improving their security position" as "prosaic" (p. 25, emphasis added). Two points are noteworthy. First, Lalman and Newman offer no formal theory; it is an empirical paper motivated by prior theoretical research, so its inclusion by Walt seems odd. Second, their empirical results pose a puzzle: there are many alliances that are not security seeking. Morrow's investigation of the trade-off between security and autonomy in alliances was partially motivated by Lalman and Newman's observation that 12 percent of nations in alliances expected to lose security as a

---

23. Recent surveys include James D. Morrow, "Leaders, States, and International Politics," in Eun Ho Lee and Woosang Kim, eds., *Recasting International Relations Paradigms* (Seoul: Korean Association of International Studies, 1996), pp. 79–101; Morrow, "The Strategic Setting of Choices: Signaling, Commitment, and Negotiation in International Politics," in David A. Lake and Robert Powell, eds., *Strategic Choice and International Relations* (Princeton, N.J.: Princeton University Press, 1999), pp. 77–114, particularly pp. 103–112; and Morrow, "The Ongoing Game-Theoretic Revolution," in Manus I. Midlarsky, ed., *Handbook of War Studies II* (Ann Arbor: University of Michigan Press, forthcoming).
24. James D. Morrow, "Capabilities, Uncertainty, and Resolve," *American Journal of Political Science*, Vol. 33, No. 4 (November 1989), pp. 941–972.
25. David Lalman, and David Newman, "Alliance Formation and National Security," *International Interactions*, Vol. 16, No. 4 (1990), pp. 239–254.

consequence of the alliance.[26] As discussed earlier, Morrow's study led to significant new insights about alliance formation, duration, and termination.

EXAMPLE NO. 5. James D. Morrow, "Alliances, Credibility, and Peacetime Costs."[27] Walt admits that "Morrow's formulation challenges the idea that alliance credibility is largely driven by concerns about reputation" (p. 25) but goes on to argue that "the conclusions for the most part echo the conventional wisdom" (pp. 25–26). Far from being a deficiency, this is an example of the power of rational choice models. Morrow has constructed a model that echoes some conventional wisdom while showing that other parts of received knowledge, specifically the presumed need to invoke international reputation, are not needed to render alliances credible. In a single model, Morrow shows the logical basis for supporting some conventional insights and for refuting others.

EXAMPLE NO. 7. James D. Fearon, "Rationalist Explanations for War."[28] Walt's characterization is mistaken in two fundamental ways. First, Walt depicts Fearon's description of the commitment problem as "merely to give a new label to a well-established idea" (p. 28). This is incorrect. The conventional argument for why anarchy leads to war—the "well-established idea"—is that there is no supranational authority to enforce agreements. Fearon notes that the absence of a central authority does not explain why states choose war over negotiated settlement. Instead, Fearon says, "the fact that under anarchy one state's efforts to make itself more secure can have the undesired but unavoidable effect of making another state less secure. . . . says nothing about the availability or feasibility of peaceful bargains that would avoid the costs of war."[29] The conventional arguments about anarchy have not adequately considered, as Fearon has, that rivals can resolve disputes peacefully to avoid costs without the aid of a central authority. Conventional arguments about anarchy are insufficient to explain the failure of negotiations to avoid war. As will be evident when we turn to Walt's critique of *War and Reason*, the recognition of commitment problems in bargaining leads to propositions that contradict realist claims about international politics.

Second, as Walt recognizes in footnote 62, "Unlike some forms of secrecy (such as number of weapons, for example), 'private information' includes information (such as a player's level of resolve) that could not be reliably

---

26. Morrow, "Alliances and Asymmetry," p. 906.
27. James D. Morrow, "Alliances, Credibility, and Peacetime Costs," *Journal of Conflict Resolution*, Vol. 38, No. 2 (June 1994), pp. 270–297.
28. James D. Fearon, "Rationalist Explanations for War," *International Organization*, Vol. 49, No. 3 (Summer 1995), pp. 379–414. Walt mistakenly refers to this paper as "Rationalist Theories of War."
29. Ibid., pp. 384–385.

revealed to the other side even if one wanted to" (p. 28), yet Walt maintains in the body of the text that "although the concept of 'private information' is broader than the more familiar idea of 'secrecy,' its effects on crisis bargaining are essentially the same" (p. 28). The effects are quite different exactly because even efforts to truthfully reveal private information may be construed by the opponent as lies or bluff, whereas secrets can be truthfully revealed and accepted as such by the other side. Incentives to misrepresent private information complicate crisis bargaining even for those inclined to be honest in ways not fully appreciated previously.

EXAMPLE NO. 10. Bruce Bueno de Mesquita and David Lalman, *War and Reason: Domestic and International Imperatives.*[30] Walt contends that the results of Bueno de Mesquita and Lalman's model are trivial in the sense that they are well known. By our count, nineteen of at least twenty-five explicit propositions are novel. Twelve of the nineteen and several of the others are tested against evidence, and none of the novel hypotheses are discussed by Walt. For instance, Bueno de Mesquita and Lalman show conditions under which extreme weakness makes countries more belligerent. Their pacific dove hypothesis—under uncertainty, very peace-loving, weak states are especially likely to respond to threats by attacking—contradicts views articulated by most realists, yet the evidence is consistent with this hypothesis. Additionally, Bueno de Mesquita and Lalman show how a commitment problem can, without uncertainty, lead to war even though all actors prefer negotiation. This result, also identified by Fearon as discussed above, is supported by the evidence.[31] The theoretical result and tests contradict Waltz's claim that uncertainty always increases the risk of instability and also contradict Robert Keohane's contention that improved information always promotes cooperation.[32]

Walt claims that Bueno de Mesquita and Lalman conclude trivially that "if both sides would rather talk than fight and if both sides know this, they do

---

30. Bruce Bueno de Mesquita and David Lalman, *War and Reason: Domestic and International Imperatives* (New Haven, Conn.: Yale University Press, 1992).

31. Fearon, "Rationalist Explanations for War."

32. Waltz, *Theory of International Politics*, p. 170; and Robert O. Keohane, *After Hegemony: Cooperation and Discord in the World Political Economy* (Princeton, N.J.: Princeton University Press, 1984), pp. 245–247. Curtis S. Signorino's test in "Strategic Interaction and the Statistical Analysis of International Conflict," *American Political Science Review,* Vol. 93, No. 2 (June 1999), pp. 279–297, contains corrected empirical tests of the paper Walt (p. 38 n. 96) cites. Signorino shows that, because of measurement—not theoretical—difficulties in *War and Reason*, the theory fares modestly at worst and at best does well. Alastair Smith, "Strategic Estimation in International Relations," paper presented at the annual meeting of the American Political Science Association, Boston, Massachusetts, September 3–6, 1998, uses a demanding Bayesian test. He finds that the international interaction game is the only theory of conflict whose predictions outperform the null hypothesis.

not fight" (p. 36 n. 93). This is incorrect. The point of *War and Reason* is to explain when nations wage war and when reason prevails so that war is averted. In *War and Reason,* all players are assumed to prefer to talk rather than wage war, and this is assumed to be common knowledge.[33] Nevertheless, the game shows conditions under which war takes place even though everyone prefers to talk (negotiate) rather than wage war. Additionally, *War and Reason* shows when doves will not fight one another and when they will; it shows when hawks will not fight one another and when they will; and it shows when hawks and doves will live peacefully or will fight one another. The propositions are contingent, and all are equally burdened by the assumption that all players know that everyone would rather talk than wage war.

Walt (p. 37 n. 95) suggests that the empirical results in *War and Reason* are not replicable because the method for measuring variables is not explained. The measurement of the primitive components of every variable are explained in the appendix so that anyone can reconstruct the composite variables. All of *War and Reason* has been replicated by others, including extensions to new or enlarged data sets. Indeed, D. Scott Bennett and Allan Stam have constructed a web site for those who wish to experiment with the replicated variables from *War and Reason* on new data sets.[34]

The case studies in *War and Reason* critiqued by Walt are used only to illustrate the intuition behind the model's logic and not as evidence. That book relies on large-N statistical studies because the hypotheses deduced from the theory are about *variation* across cases.[35] Prediction of individual cases is not the appropriate way to test the propositions in *War and Reason.* Space limitations preclude addressing Walt's criticisms of individual case illustrations, each of which is readily defended.

Relevant Knowledge

Walt's concluding remarks contend that "instead of using their expertise to address important real-world problems, academics often focus on narrow and trivial problems that may impress their colleagues but are of little practical

---

33. "ASSUMPTION 4: *All nations prefer to resolve their differences through negotiation rather than war.*" See Bueno de Mesquita and Lalman, *War and Reason,* p. 40 (emphasis in original).
34. Their EUGene software, data, and documentation can be found at http://wizard.ucr.edu/cps/eugene/menu.html.
35. Because of the difficulty in estimating values for key variables, tests evaluate whether the *central tendency* of the data supports the propositions. The tests all support the theoretical claims in Bueno de Mesquita and Lalman, *War and Reason,* pp. 76 n. 10, 84, 88, 90, 112–114, 127–128, 133–134, 157, 190–191, 195–197, 205–208, 215–216, and especially 280.

value" (p. 46). In this section, we explain our view of the relationship between basic science and policy engineering and point to a development from formal models that has proven of immense practical value in the policy world.

We share Walt's view that social science should inform public policy. To inform public policy effectively, advice should be based on careful logical and empirical foundations. Basic research, whether through formal modeling or other methodologies, is necessary to establish such foundations. Social engineering based on personal wisdom, judgment, or taste alone fails to provide a framework for determining appropriate policy responses under changing circumstances. Results grounded in careful science are much less subject to idiosyncratic variations in tastes.

We believe that basic science uncovers general principles that are useful for informing decisions about current problems, even though the purpose of basic science is not immediately directed at the policy arena. Science should, in our view, drive policy engineering; basic science should not be driven by policy concerns. The focus of basic research is the discovery of general principles. Thus we should not be surprised that there can be a long interlude between scientific discoveries and their practical application.

Given the short history of formal models in international relations, it is encouraging that this literature has already produced a practical tool for policy analysis—Bueno de Mesquita's "expected utility" model, sometimes referred to as Policon or as Factions—derived from basic research.[36] This computerized model predicts the outcome of complex political settings, including detailed forecasts of actor-specific actions. Used as a simulation tool, it allows the design of strategies to improve the chances of achieving desired ends. These strategies are detailed, dynamic, and practical. The model leads to specific policy advice and has an independently documented track record of accuracy and precision. Real-time predictions from this model are in the academic literature.[37] The

---

36. The applied model grows out of Bruce Bueno de Mesquita, *The War Trap* (New Haven, Conn.: Yale University Press, 1981); Bueno de Mesquita, "An Expected Utility Explanation of Conflict Escalation," in Dina Zinnes, ed., *Conflict Processes and the Breakdown of International Systems*, Denver Monograph Series in World Affairs, vol. 20, bk. 2 (Denver: University of Denver, 1983), pp. 47–60; Bueno de Mesquita, "The War Trap Revisited," *American Political Science Review*, Vol. 79, No. 1 (March 1985), pp. 157–176; Bueno de Mesquita, David Newman, and Alvin Rabushka, *Forecasting Political Events* (New Haven, Conn.: Yale University Press, 1985); and Bueno de Mesquita and Frans Stokman, eds., *European Community Decision Making* (New Haven, Conn.: Yale University Press, 1992).
37. Bueno de Mesquita, Newman, and Rabushka, *Forecasting Political Events*; Bruce Bueno de Mesquita, "Multilateral Negotiations: A Spatial Analysis of the Arab-Israeli Dispute," *International Organization*, Vol. 44, No. 3 (Summer 1990), pp. 317–340; Bueno de Mesquita and A.F.K. Organski, "A Mark in Time Saves *Nein*," *International Political Science Review*, Vol. 13, No. 1 (January 1992),

reader can judge the accuracy and value of the model from reading these articles. Some examples include predictions about the succession to Ayatollah Khomeini in Iran (published five years before his death), North and South Korea's entry into the United Nations, and Yasser Arafat's willingness to accept a very limited concession over land from Israel in exchange for a peace accord (published in 1990).

Others have evaluated the accuracy of the model's predictions in the academic literature. James Ray and Bruce Russett note that "this 'expected utility' forecasting model has now been tried and tested extensively. The amount of publicly available information and evidence regarding this model and the accuracy of its forecasts is sufficiently substantial, it seems to us, to make it deserving of serious consideration as a 'scientific' enterprise."[38]

The United States government also reports that it finds the model accurate and that it uses the model to assist with important foreign policy matters. According to Stanley Feder, of the Central Intelligence Agency, the model was "found to be accurate about 90 percent of the time." Feder reports that "forecasts and analyses using Policon have proved to be significantly more precise and detailed than traditional analyses. Additionally, a number of predictions based on Policon have contradicted those made by the intelligence community, nearly always represented by the analysts who provided the input data. In every case, the Policon forecasts proved to be correct."[39]

---

pp. 81–100; Bueno de Mesquita, James D. Morrow, and Samuel S.G. Wu, "Forecasting the Risks of Nuclear Proliferation: Taiwan as an Illustration of the Method," *Security Studies*, Vol. 2, Nos. 3–4 (Spring/Summer 1993), pp. 311–331; Bueno de Mesquita and Stokman, *European Community Decision Making*; Wu and Bueno de Mesquita, "Assessing the Dispute in the South China Sea: A Model of China's Security Decision Making," *International Studies Quarterly*, Vol. 38, No. 3 (September 1994), pp. 379–403; Bueno de Mesquita, David Newman, and Alvin Rabushka, *Red Flag over Hong Kong* (Chatham, N.J.: Chatham House, 1996); Bueno de Mesquita and Yi Feng, "Forecasting China's Political and Economic Future," *Problems of Post-Communism*, Vol. 44, No. 2 (March–April 1997), pp. 14–27; Bueno de Mesquita, "The End of the Cold War: Predicting an Emergent Property," *Journal of Conflict Resolution*, Vol. 42, No. 2 (April 1998), pp. 131–155; Roberto Ley-Borrás, "Forecasts and Decisions on Economic Pacts in Mexico," *Annals of the American Academy of Political and Social Science*, Vol. 550 (March 1997), pp. 85–95; Bueno de Mesquita, "Forecasting Policy Decisions: An Expected Utility Approach to Post-Khomeini Iran," *PS*, Vol. 17, No. 2 (Spring 1984), pp. 226–236; Bueno de Mesquita and Chae-Han Kim, "Prospects for a New Regional Order in Northeast Asia," *Korean Journal of Defense Analysis*, Vol. 3, No. 2 (Winter 1991), pp. 65–82; and an entire special issue of *International Interactions*, Vol. 13, No. 2 (Fall 1997), edited by Jacek Kugler and Yi Feng, as well as more than a dozen articles not listed here.

38. James L. Ray and Bruce M. Russett, "The Future as Arbiter of Theoretical Controversies: Predictions, Explanations, and the End of the Cold War," *British Journal of Political Science*, Vol. 25, No. 4 (October 1996), p. 1569. See also William McGurn, "We Warned You," *Far Eastern Economic Review*, June 13, 1996, p. 68.

39. Stanley A. Feder, "Factions and Policon: New Ways to Analyze Politics," in H. Bradford Westerfield, ed., *Inside CIA's Private World: Declassified Articles from the Agency's Internal Journal, 1955–1992* (New Haven, Conn.: Yale University Press, 1995), pp. 274–292, at pp. 275, 292.

Feder discusses a few applications in depth while enumerating many others. Analysts have used the model to examine economic, social, and political issues. They have dealt with routine policy decisions and with questions threatening the survival of particular regimes. Issues have spanned a variety of cultural settings, economic systems, and political systems. For instance, the model helped keep Taiwan in the Asian Development Bank when China entered, and it identified important, previously undetected weaknesses in the coalition backing Ferdinand Marcos in the Philippines. Feder's discussion makes clear that the model provides added insights and real value above and beyond the knowledge of the experts who provide the data.

The extensive use of this model by the government of the United States is further documented by a story reported in *Izvestia*. Officials from the U.S. government demonstrated the model to Russian journalists and Russian intelligence officials. *Izvestia* reported on what it was told: "Experts engaging in studies within the framework of this system state that on the basis of long experience of using it, it can be said with a great degree of confidence that the forecasts are highly accurate. In particular, according to them, the 'Factions' method was used in May 1991 to predict the August putsch. . . . The forecasts are given to the President, Congress, and the U.S. government and are a substantial factor influencing the elaboration of the country's foreign policy course."[40]

Several aspects of the model just discussed are important to understand our view of how basic science informs policy. First, the model uses the results of basic research. That research was not designed to address specific policy problems; it strove to understand the general properties of political conflict. Second, one cannot know in advance which basic research will prove fruitful for policymaking. To judge basic research in general because most fails to make an immediate contribution to public policy is to abandon the prospect of having scientifically grounded policy analysis. Third, the model discussed here does not express policy opinions or make normative judgments. It elucidates feasible paths to chosen outcomes; it does not suggest what outcomes should be desired. Fourth, the model is general across cases. It always uses the identical computerized analysis to specify how variables relate to one another. Only the data vary from case study to case study. Fifth, the model required extensive engineering to convert abstract research results into a practical policy tool. We should be clear that theory should not be expected to jump directly

---

40. "Russia Is Doomed to Stability Consider American Experts," *Izvestia*, April 3, 1995.

into policy applications. Much hard engineering work needs to be done following equally hard scientific work.

Conclusion

An anonymous political scientist once explained to an economist the difference between their fields as follows: "In economics, you have *The Wealth of Nations;* in political science we have a wealth of notions." We have tried to lay out some of the advantages of using formal theory to sort through the wealth of notions in the field of international politics. The criteria for judging scientific theories, on which we and Walt agree, require logical consistency and empirical validity. We believe that logical consistency is the gatekeeper for judging theories; a theory that contains logical inconsistencies must be remedied before it can have any empirical content. The criteria of logical consistency and empirical validity are how a scientific field sorts through a wealth of notions.

Formal models assist this sorting by helping the research community examine the logical consistency of arguments. Of course, formalism is not necessary for close examination of the logic of an argument. We have found models helpful, particularly in dealing precisely with the details of arguments. As we have shown, Walt's article at times misrepresents the arguments advanced in papers using formal models. The details matter, and models have helped us establish both the details of an argument and their consequences for the conclusions of the argument.

Walt's article also appears to suffer from some confusion about the scientific enterprise. Scientists specialize across the research community. Some physicists, for example, are theorists and others are experimentalists. Yet Walt criticizes modeling papers that do not contain immediate empirical tests of their propositions even when he knows that other papers test implications of those models.[41] Both logical analysis and empirical assessment are essential for the advancement of science. They need not be done by the same people at the same time.

---

41. Walt criticizes James D. Fearon, "Domestic Audience Costs and the Escalation of International Disputes," *American Political Science Review,* Vol. 88, No. 3 (September 1994), pp. 577–592, for not containing a direct test (pp. 34–35). Yet Walt also notes in footnote 86 (p. 34) that Joe Eyerman and Robert A. Hart Jr. test Fearon's prediction in "An Empirical Test of the Audience Cost Proposition: Democracy Speaks Louder Than Words," *Journal of Conflict Resolution,* Vol. 40, No. 4 (December 1996), pp. 597–616.

We have tried to clarify our views about the contributions of formal theory to security studies. Through examples we have shown how logical rigor has helped clarify arguments. We have explored briefly some of the novel insights that the formal literature, though still in its infancy, has already contributed. And we have demonstrated that the formal literature has made an important contribution to public policy. We conclude, then, by agreeing with Walt that "security studies should welcome contributions from formal theory" (p. 48).

The Contributions of Rational Choice: A Defense of Pluralism

Lisa L. Martin

In "Rigor or Rigor Mortis? Rational Choice and Security Studies," Stephen Walt warns of the dangers to the field of security studies that are in store "if formal theory were to dominate security studies as it has other areas of political science."[1] He backs up these warnings by evaluating published formal work in the field according to seemingly reasonable criteria, finding that the gain in rigor inherent in formal work is not sufficient to offset its empirical, creative, and policy-relevance weaknesses. Although Walt ends with a plea for diversity (p. 48), the overall structure of his argument puts rational choice on trial, finds it lacking yet threatening to become dominant, and does little to serve the purpose of encouraging pluralism.

As a consumer rather than producer of sophisticated formal theory, I find Walt's critique of formal work off target and his worries about its imminent hegemony unfounded. My own work, as well as that of many other scholars, has benefited enormously from the theorizing of those who have better technical skills and the ability to work through complex mathematical models. The field of security studies would be severely impoverished if formal work were discouraged.

In this response, I make three arguments. The first is to highlight a signal strength of formal work that Walt neglects: its ability to generate linked, coherent sets of propositions and insights. Walt's analysis focuses entirely on individual, isolated hypotheses, finding them lacking in originality, empirical support, or policy relevance. This approach misses the importance of theory in providing insights that are logically connected to one another in an integrated analytical framework, a necessary condition for progress in social science. Second, I address the benefits of formalizing the insights of informal

Lisa L. Martin is Professor of Government at Harvard University. She is the author of Democratic Commitments: Legislatures and International Cooperation (Princeton, N.J.: Princeton University Press, forthcoming).

I would like to thank Celeste Wallander and Barbara Walter for discussions and comments on this piece, and Lawrence Hamlet for his able research assistance.

1. Stephen M. Walt, "Rigor or Rigor Mortis? Rational Choice and Security Studies," *International Security*, Vol. 23, No. 4 (Spring 1999), pp. 5–48, at p. 46. Further references appear in parentheses in the text.

International Security, Vol. 24, No. 2 (Fall 1999), pp. 74–83
© 1999 by the President and Fellows of Harvard College and the Massachusetts Institute of Technology.

rational choice—the generic "Didn't Schelling already say that?" question. These benefits can be summarized as providing specificity to propositions and identifying the contingency of many hypotheses. Third, I address the "dominance" issue by looking at the numbers of articles published in leading journals between 1994 and 1998 that use sophisticated formal models. This review shows that there is no apparent danger of formal work becoming dominant in the field of security studies, calling the need for warnings such as Walt's into question. Better empirical testing of formal models is surely desirable—as is better empirical work in international relations and security studies in general. Singling out formal modeling as a threat to the field, however, is unfounded and does nothing to encourage diversity.

Coherence

The approach that Walt takes in his review of formal models is to single out particular hypotheses and propositions that have been derived in prominent examples of formal work. He argues that, taken individually, none of these insights is valuable enough to justify the technical complexity that went into producing them. I leave it to those authors who were singled out to respond directly to these claims, if they desire.

The point I wish to make here is a larger one, however. The value of formal theory, like any theory, does not lie primarily in its ability to generate isolated propositions, however original or empirically valid such assertions might be. Generating isolated propositions does not require a theoretical framework at all, much less the relatively elaborate framework of mathematical game theory. Any thoughtful observer of international affairs is likely to be able to generate a good insight here or there.

Social science, in contrast, relies on theory. The reason is fundamental to the drive to make social science a progressive, cumulative effort. Proving or refuting an isolated proposition has some value. But without an overarching analytical framework that generates *complexes* of related propositions, determining the empirical validity of a particular proposition is a dead end rather than a step toward cumulative knowledge. Social science does not consist simply of compiling lists of propositions and a tally of which are true, false, or undecided. Instead, it contributes to human knowledge by showing how sets of related propositions are tied to an underlying set of core assumptions and methods of analyzing social interaction. When a framework exists that ties together coherent sets of assumptions and propositions, one strong empirical finding, positive or negative, has myriad implications. It is this multiplier effect that makes theorizing worthwhile and creates at least the possibility of cumulative knowledge.

This vision of embedded complexes of assumptions and propositions is common to any positivist philosophy of social science, and Walt's style of analysis makes clear that he is a positivist. I share this prejudice. But without an emphasis on theory, empirical testing of propositions can degenerate into a crudely inductive enterprise that is quickly made valueless by the next change of fortune in the practice of international politics. When propositions are tied together, whether in a Lakatosian research program or Kuhnian paradigm, as a set of insights that are commonly derived from coherent assumptions, empirical evidence on one insight leads to updating and deeper understanding of the others. It also contributes to our sense of whether the underlying set of assumptions is a good tool for making sense of the world. We lose this more holistic contribution—the notion that the whole is greater than the sum of its parts—if we neglect the value of an integrated analytical framework. Evaluating a theory only in terms of its ability to generate isolated new, empirically proven, and policy-relevant propositions is akin to stripping a car for parts. One is left without a vehicle that can go anywhere, just a pile of unconnected scrap.

If we can agree on the value of integrated theoretical frameworks for promoting deeper understanding and progress in security studies, the next question is whether formal modeling has any benefits when it comes to providing such an integrated framework. While I do not deny that other methods have the capacity to generate integrated complexes of assumptions, insights, and testable propositions, formal work must be rated very high by this standard. It provides a deductive, logically coherent method for relating assumptions and hypotheses to each other. It forces researchers to make their assumptions explicit, and provides a tool for understanding the extent to which hypotheses are robust or highly sensitive to particular assumptions. It exposes logical flaws in more informal arguments that can degrade their ability to generate coherent complexes of insights. It also creates the potential for different fields within the social sciences to speak to one another. Firmer integration of security studies within the discipline of political science is encouraged by the use of formal methods.[2]

As an example of the contributions of formal work, take the literature on reputation and credibility. Walt reviews a number of articles based on this

---

2. My thanks to Celeste Wallander for suggesting this point.

literature, extracting a few propositions from each of them. He derides each of these propositions as a reinvention of the wheel, confirmation of what we already know, or simply not a big deal. Many of these assertions could be questioned on their own terms. More important, however, is that by focusing only on these specific propositions we miss the larger picture that is created by formal analyses of reputation and credibility. This larger picture ties together understandings about the role of uncertainty; the importance of initial beliefs; the dynamics and outcomes of updating beliefs; the selection of deterrent or challenging strategies; the availability of actions that impose differential costs on different types of actors; the importance of a common-knowledge framework in which to interpret signals about resolve; the significance of repetition and the shadow of the future; the likelihood of success for different strategies; the ability of different types of actors to mimic one another or bluff; and others.

Some of these insights make up the direct implications of a model—that is, what it was designed to illuminate in the first place. Others are indirect implications of the same models. The important point here is that a *set* of direct and indirect implications flow from any particular model. The process of empirical validation, or application to particular policy challenges, should take into account the integrated nature of these implications. A strong positive or negative finding on any particular proposition has implications for many others, and for the assumptions that drove the model in the first place. The act of formalization therefore dramatically increases the empirical leverage researchers can apply, and provides direction to research efforts that is lacking if research is treated as simply going down a laundry list of propositions.

Specificity and Contingency

Walt raises a concern that I hear repeated frequently by graduate students and colleagues in many different settings. I think of this as the generic "Didn't Schelling already say that?" question. The point of this critique is to show that informal analysts of strategy have been able to produce insight without the benefit of mathematics. Walt hopes to differentiate between informal and sophisticated formal versions of rationalist analysis, putting a high value on the former but criticizing the latter. If Thomas Schelling and Albert Wohlstetter could generate deep insights, the argument goes, what is the value in using more sophisticated mathematical techniques? There are many answers to this question, but here I single out a few of the most general.

The first was summarized in the previous section. Although informal theorizing about strategy has led to important insights, formalizing these insights provides an overarching analytical framework that is valuable in many ways. It suggests new propositions and shows how propositions are related to one another. It forces the analyst to make assumptions and conditions more explicit. In short, it provides a logic of analysis that allows for more reliable progress in our social-scientific endeavors.

Second, any claim that Schelling or Wohlstetter came to their conclusions without being influenced by formal mathematical approaches is totally unfounded. Wohlstetter's background, for example, was in operations research and systems analysis, both highly mathematical and technically complex fields. Although it is true that Wohlstetter had a genius for translating mathematical insights into (relatively) plain English in his RAND studies, this is not to say that he could have produced these studies if deprived of his mathematical background. Many of us who work in the rationalist tradition, but do not spend much time developing our own sophisticated models, are in a similar situation. Our theories and propositions have been deeply influenced by the more technical work of others, and this debt should be made more explicit rather than dismissed. Tracing the chain of causation to show the impact, or nonimpact, of mathematical reasoning on informal studies of strategy would require much deeper analysis than Walt provides. The fact that some good papers on strategy do not themselves include formal models by no means demonstrates that formal modeling made no contribution to these papers.

Third, and the major point I wish to make in this section, formalization adds specificity and contingency to the claims that authors such as Schelling have made. Many of the propositions Schelling advances are brilliant and intuitively plausible. Unfortunately, he also at times advances precisely the opposite proposition, and it appears equally brilliant and plausible. The difficulty here is not that either proposition is wrong. It is that the propositions are often stated without the degree of specificity that is necessary to evaluate their logical or empirical validity, or that they are true only under particular unspecified conditions. Formalization greatly increases specificity, and few methods are better for specifying the conditions under which particular propositions hold. As scientific fields, natural or social, develop, they invariably become more mathematical.[3] This is not the result of a conspiracy of the mathematically

---

3. Walt approvingly cites Darwin's theory of evolution to demonstrate that seminal theories in the natural sciences are not always mathematical (p. 16). But this claim neglects the fact that evolutionary biology has developed substantially since Darwin and in some areas has become highly mathematical.

gifted or a guildlike attempt to exclude outsiders. It is in part because math provides the tools to sort out apparently conflicting claims by specifying the conditions under which they hold. Using mathematical tools is a method for adding specificity and contingency to the seminal claims of informal theorists.

To take one example, consider Schelling's influential analyses of the problem of credibility in *The Strategy of Conflict* and *Arms and Influence*.[4] In *Strategy and Conflict*, we find one of Schelling's most cited ideas: tight constraints on negotiators that result from domestic politics can enhance credibility and prove an asset in international bargaining. According to Schelling, "If the executive branch negotiates under legislative authority, with its position constrained by law, and it is evident that Congress will not be reconvened to change the law within the necessary time period, then the executive branch has a firm position that is visible to its negotiating partners."[5] In *Arms and Influence*, Schelling argues that "the centralization of decision" and "the divorce of war from political processes"[6] enhance the credibility of the threat to use nuclear weapons once war has begun.

On their face, these two claims appear to contradict each other. It is obvious, however, that Schelling is considering two very different settings in coming to these apparently contradictory statements. It seems entirely plausible that at times decentralized political processes are likely to enhance credibility, while at other times centralization will be an asset. It is difficult, however, to sort out the conditions under which one statement versus the other is true without more carefully specifying assumptions and working through a formal assessment of the credibility of threats under different conditions of strategic interaction, iteration, beliefs and capacities of other actors, and so on. In other words, formalization would allow us to move toward the conditional propositions about credibility that are implied by Schelling's analysis. In addition, it is possible that what exactly is meant by "credibility" differs in these two examples. Precisely defining credibility and adding specificity to the propositions above could constitute another justification for formalizing Schelling's ideas.

One could perform the same kind of analysis for Schelling's discussions of costless communication (what we would today call "cheap talk") and costly moves. Developments in modern game theory have led to a much better

---

4. Thomas C. Schelling, *The Strategy of Conflict* (Cambridge, Mass.: Harvard University Press, 1980); and Schelling, *Arms and Influence* (New Haven, Conn.: Yale University Press, 1966).
5. Schelling, *Strategy of Conflict*, p. 28.
6. Schelling, *Arms and Influence*, p. 20.

understanding of the conditions under which cheap talk can make a difference for outcomes, and when costly signals can. Similarly, Schelling's discussion of the qualitative nature of useful focal points versus the benefits of randomization (a quantitative concept) could perhaps be sorted out and developed into testable propositions via the application of formal methods.

None of the above should be taken as a criticism of early informal analyses of strategy. These analyses were indeed seminal, and continue to influence policy and research today. The point of a "seminal" idea, however, is precisely that it stimulates future work, leading later analysts to refine and develop the initial idea. Using formal methods to pursue such development is often a highly productive enterprise, as it allows analysts to specify ideas more precisely and to make contingent claims about the conditions under which particular relationships should hold. Pointing out that those who use mathematical approaches are often building on the seminal ideas of informal analysts by no means undermines the value of formal methods. Instead, it suggests that standard procedures of scientific progress are being applied.

The Role of Formal Theory in Security Studies

One of the more disturbing aspects of Walt's article is the sense of imminent danger that it assumes and attempts to spread. The article contains repeated references to what would happen if formal theory were to take over the field. I am a committed proponent of diversity. Different approaches have different strengths and weaknesses. The field of security studies has by no means yet approached the status of "normal science," where one particular approach has proven its superiority and is commonly used by most researchers.

If the point is to encourage pluralism and tolerance, an attack on one particular approach must be based on the presumption that it is overrepresented. This is one issue where we can benefit from examining some concrete facts. How prevalent is the use of sophisticated formal models in security studies? Is it prevalent enough that concerns about its impending dominance are justified?

To answer this question, I undertook a survey of articles on international security issues published in the leading journals in the field between 1994 and 1998. I then calculated the percentage of articles that presented a formal model, using Walt's definition.[7] Table 1 presents these results.

---

7. Walt (p. 9) narrows his analysis to scholarship that uses "specific mathematical models" to identify equilibrium outcomes. He excludes analyses that merely draw on game-theoretic concepts.

Table 1. Articles on International Security with a Formal Model, 1994–98.

Journal	Number of Security Articles	Number of Formal Articles	Percentage of Formal Articles
American Political Science Review	26	8	30.8
International Organization	43	5	11.6
International Security	113	0	0
International Studies Quarterly	83	11	13.3
Journal of Conflict Resolution	152	42	27.6
Security Studies	105	0	0
World Politics	21	5	23.8
Total	**543**	**71**	**13.1**

In collecting the data for Table 1, I used the following rules. I assumed that all of the articles in *International Security*, the *Journal of Conflict Resolution*, and *Security Studies* counted as studies of international security. This rule probably led to an overcounting of the number of formal articles, because some of the formal articles published in the *Journal of Conflict Resolution* are pure game theory, without application to a particular issue, or are on areas of conflict other than international security. However, to avoid making judgment calls that could result in undercounting formal articles, I treated the entire journal as being about security issues. I eliminated publications that were book reviews or exchanges with authors; again, including these would have reduced the percentage of publications that were formal. Following Walt's lead, I did not include as formal articles those that drew informally on ideas such as the prisoners' dilemma or mixed strategies.

As Table 1 shows, more than 500 articles were published in these seven journals in this five-year span. Of these articles, 71, or 13.1 percent, presented a formal model.[8] Looking at the breakdown by journal, we see that 42 out of these 71—nearly 60 percent—were published in just one journal, the *Journal of Conflict Resolution*. The journal has clearly selected a niche for itself, becoming by far the most common outlet for formal work in security studies. The other two journals that specialize in security studies, *International Security* and *Secu-*

---

8. One could argue that acceptance rates would be more revealing than publication rates. Such data were not available on short notice, however. In addition, because authors rationally choose where to submit their manuscripts, any data on acceptance rates would be subject to severe selection bias.

rity Studies, have not published a single article using a formal model in the last five years. The less specialized journals show variation in the percentage of security articles they publish that use a formal model. This figure ranges from a low of 11.6 percent for *International Organization*[9] to a high of 30.8 percent for the *American Political Science Review.*

Looking at these figures, it is hard to work up much of a sense of urgency about the impending dominance of formal work in security studies, or to support a claim that those who do not do formal work are becoming "marginalized" (p. 7). Outside of the *Journal of Conflict Resolution,* fewer than 30 articles using a formal model have been published in the last five years. Overall, formal modeling remains a small piece in the fragmented universe of security studies. Given these numbers, and the contributions of formal modeling discussed above, it seems more appropriate to encourage formal work than to broadcast warnings about how its dominance might doom the field.

Conclusion

Walt's article has raised a series of challenges to those who produce sophisticated formal work in security studies. While presenting these challenges as a plea for diversity and tolerance, Walt adopts an approach that is likely to generate just the opposite: conflict, defensiveness, and countercharges. Many of Walt's claims are stated in comparative terms—for example, that empirical work to test formal models is weaker than that to test other approaches, or that formal models have less policy relevance than do other models. None of the analysis undertaken, however, is at all comparative. Three criteria are specified—logical consistency, creativity, and empirical validity—but in the end, no formal model is held to be valuable unless it makes a direct contribution to policy debates, regardless of its logical consistency relative to other approaches.[10] In other words, these three criteria are by no means weighted

---

9. It is somewhat surprising that *International Organization* has published 43 articles on security in this period, considering that it is usually understood as primarily an international political economy journal.
10. After admitting that formal methods encourage precision and logical consistency, Walt dismisses these criteria as not demonstrating "the superiority of formal techniques over other approaches" (p. 20). But surely they would imply superiority, all else being equal. One can only conclude that precision and consistency in practice receive little weight in Walt's calculation. In addition, Walt does not address how internally inconsistent and logically incomplete propositions can make a positive contribution to policy debates, except by stimulating others to do better.

equally, and they are not applied in a systematic manner to alternative approaches in security studies.

The most basic weaknesses of Walt's broadside, however, lie not in his specific arguments, but in errors of omission and in unsubstantiated presumptions. Errors of omission lie in the criteria chosen for evaluating theories. Two criteria that would have worked in favor of formal models are neglected. The first is the capacity of an approach to generate integrated, coherent complexes of assumptions and propositions. Extracting a few isolated propositions from models and deriding them for being insufficiently original or proven misses this essential characteristic of a progressive research agenda. The second is the ability to add the necessary elements of specificity and contingency to individual propositions to allow for accurate assessments of their empirical validity. Informal analyses of strategy have provided numerous brilliant insights, but they are often contradicted by their equally brilliant opposites. Formalization provides a technique for sorting out these apparent inconsistencies.

Finally, the presumption that formal work is becoming a prerequisite for publication in security studies, or is in any way threatening to become dominant, has no foundation in fact. A survey of articles on security published in the leading professional journals between 1994 and 1998 shows that only 13 percent of published articles present a formal model, and that nearly 60 percent of those that do have come out in just one journal. Given this reality, the claim that a wide-ranging attack on the contributions of formal models is in fact a plea for tolerance seems disingenuous.

Return of the Luddites

*Emerson M.S. Niou
and
Peter D. Ordeshook*

In this response to Stephen Walt's critique[1] of the application of formal analysis to international security studies, we take strong issue with a number of Walt's arguments and assertions, and we try to clarify what we believe are his misconceptions about the nature and mechanisms of progress in scientific research. We begin, however, by identifying some of the issues we do not dispute with Walt. First, it is true that formal analysis, especially in the area of security studies, is only infrequently motivated by the attempt to explain some well-documented empirical regularity or universally recognized empirical anomaly. If there is room for disagreement here, it is the extent to which regularities or anomalies can be found in the security studies literature that are sufficiently precise to allow careful analysis. Second, there is little disagreement that some formalism exists for its own sake, although we need to be cautious here because much of this rigor seeks to understand the very definition of rationality in complex strategic environments. Third, despite the proliferation of competing models of deterrence, bargaining, coalitions, threats, and so on, those models are rarely set against each other for competitive empirical assessment. Finally, we cannot ignore the fact that very little of what researchers label "theory" is theory in any true sense, but instead is often best described as a demonstration of one's ability to cobble together assumptions and derive something that can be labeled "lemma" or "theorem."

Rational Choice, Game Theory, or Formalism?

Despite these agreements, we believe that much of Walt's discussion is wrongheaded and counterproductive to his objective of sustaining a policy-relevant subfield of security studies. To begin, Walt's article is not a dispassionate attempt at "evaluating the contribution of recent formal work in the field" (p. 8); rather, it is an unconstructive critique. But what is it a critique of— rational choice, game theory, or formalism? His article begins by bemoaning the limitations and increasing predominance of the rational choice paradigm

Emerson M.S. Niou is Associate Professor of Political Science at Duke University. Peter D. Ordeshook is Professor of Political Science at the California Institute of Technology.

1. Stephen M. Walt, "Rigor or Rigor Mortis? Rational Choice and Security Studies," *International Security*, Vol. 23, No. 4 (Spring 1999), pp. 5–48. Further references to this article appear in parentheses in the text.

International Security, Vol. 24, No. 2 (Fall 1999), pp. 84–96

(citing such "experts" as Chalmers Johnson). Then, via a superficial review of Bayesian analysis, Walt's focus detours to game theory, but soon is directed at three things—the paradigm, game theory, and formalism—after essentially equating the paradigm with game theory and formalism. This blurred focus is occasioned, doubtlessly, by the fact that the paradigm, game theory, and formalism, though intimately related, are not equivalent: nonmathematical scholars such as V.O. Key certainly embraced rational choice perspectives; William Riker, arguably the father (or at least midwife) of rational choice thought in political science, rarely, if ever, proved a theorem and instead relied on the formal insights of others; and the use of mathematics often falls outside the domain of what anyone might argue is rational choice theorizing.

Walt's true target, though, appears to be formalism. He gives only passing reference to the usual shopworn critiques of the rationalist paradigm (although he cannot refrain in footnote 35 on page 17 from swallowing the misconception that the paradigm presupposes people who are mathematical geniuses), and he seems only mildly discomfited by the folk theorems of game theory, which place the as yet unmodeled and poorly understood mechanisms of equilibrium selection at the center of *any* complete theory of social processes. The reason for Walt's redirected focus, we suspect, is that the study of international relations and security is a subfield of political science that has long accepted the rationalist premise of self-interested action and depended, albeit imprecisely, on the strategic imperatives of game theory (recall that much of game theory's early development was motivated by the inherent inadequacies of other modes of analysis into strategic matters). Here, of course, we need not refer only to contemporary scholars, but to our classical predecessors (e.g., Taylor, Morgenthau, Claude, etc.). Notions of rationality, self-interest, and strategy permeate these earlier writings, while debates among their heirs (e.g., Waltz, Keohane, Jervis, Gilpin, etc.) are more likely to concern individual motives, perceptions and beliefs, the role of institutions in constraining individual action, and the specification of strategic environments.

Consistency

It would seem, then, that there should be considerable room for agreement among us. Unfortunately, that room is circumscribed by Walt's failure to understand at least five aspects of scientific study: (1) the value of consistency; (2) the creativity inherent in a formal model's development; (3) the necessity of proceeding with clearly explicated null models; (4) the practical nature of assessing the empirical content of a model; and (5) the different ways in which science advances in other disciplines.

Our difficulties begin with Walt's discussion of the relative value of logical consistency and precision. Put simply, Walt stacks the deck against formal analysis by asserting that originality and empirical validity are more highly valued than are logical consistency and precision: "Although all . . . are important, the latter two criteria—originality and empirical validity—are especially prized" (p. 13). But while an argument can easily be original if it is incoherent, illogical, or imprecise, we do not see how any idea, hypothesis, or argument can be empirically valid if it is any of these things. Punch lines sustained by obscure or disconnected reasoning may be true, but only accidentally so. And how do we know they are true if their opposite cannot be refuted because we do not know what that opposite is owing to vague conceptualizations? To have content, all arguments must possess domain constraints in the form of initial assumptions, a definition of terms, and evident logical connections, and we cannot assess empirical validity if, as is the case with much of what is labeled "theory" in security studies, one or more of these things is nonexistent. To impose only the criteria of originality and the *appearance* of empirical validity establishes a field upon which the rational choice theorist quite properly rejects playing.

In the same vein, Walt laments that formal essays are difficult to read, because doing so requires wading through pages of dense notation and mathematical argument to learn the hidden assumptions and restrictions of the analysis. This lament, however, is different than Walt's assertion that "formal methods . . . make it easier to bury key assumptions within the model, thereby forcing readers to invest considerable time and effort to unearth the basic logic of the argument" (p. 20). That assumptions are sometimes less than self-evident is true. But, and this is the big "but," it is hardly an established fact that formalism makes it easier (than what?) to camouflage the logic of an argument. On the contrary, a careful reading will either uncover all assumptions or reveal their absence if the analysis is logically flawed. Walt may bemoan his difficulty with discovering or understanding assumptions that are formally stated, but to assert that they cannot be discovered by those who make the effort is patently false.

Having opted for the artful values of originality and the appearance of empirical validity, Walt fails to acknowledge fully that logical consistency, precision, and the attendant discoverability of assumptions are not uniform characteristics of much of anything else. If consistency, precision, and discoverability did characterize other less formal approaches, formalism and even the rational choice paradigm would not have gained the foothold in our discipline that so concerns Walt. It is silly to deny that a reasoned and informal contemplation of events and processes cannot yield insights that often move the focus of scientific investigation. But the rational choice paradigm and formalism are not mushrooms that sprung up in an unattended intellectual forest. They are reactions to a discipline mired in imprecision, vagueness, obscure logic, ill-defined constructs, nontestable hypotheses, and ad hoc argument. They are a reaction to a discipline that in the 1920s proclaimed the Weimar constitution the greatest political-intellectual achievement of its age; a discipline that in the 1960s substituted correlation for cause; a discipline submerged in such conveniently vague and ill-defined ideas as "power," "leadership," "authority," "group," "alliance," "function," "ideology," "culture," "regime," "stability," and "balance." They are reactions to a discipline that substituted the well-turned phrase for concrete constructs, operational measures for theoretical primitives, and the gloss of methodological sophistication for true theory. They are, in short, a reaction to a discipline that did and does precisely what Walt critiques the formal analyst of doing—burying key assumptions in an indecipherable format, although generally that format was a language more to the liking of those who studied French and Plato in college rather than calculus.

As part of his critique of the weight that formal analysts place on consistency and precision, Walt acknowledges that the limitations of the rationalist paradigm and game theory "do not discredit the use of formal models." But he then attempts to advance the argument that "the potential gains in precision and logical consistency do not demonstrate the superiority of formal techniques over other approaches" (p. 20). We might agree if we knew the identities of these other approaches. If Walt's argument is to be constructive, it is incumbent that he establish a better treatment of the specific difficulties noted by "other approaches," for as we are all taught in elementary philosophy of science courses, we reject a theory only when a better one becomes available. The questions that immediately come to mind here, of course, are: Is there a theory of risk that we can substitute for Bayesian analysis? Where in the study of international relations do we find a more coherent or empirically valid theory of strategic complexity? What other part of social science treats the indeterminacies of social processes that game theory's folk theorems uncover?

Creativity

Perhaps our sharpest disagreement with any specific point in Walt's argument, however, is his assertion that "technical sophistication and logical consistency did not yield particularly creative or original results" (p. 26). Again, this is less a coherent argument than a simple expression of prejudice, because logical consistency is itself a profoundly important creative contribution. How many trees have been cut to publish attempts at explicating Robert Keohane and Joseph Nye's synthesis of realist and liberal perspectives, Waltz's alternating conceptualizations of realism, the true content of neorealism, or, more to the point of Walt's substantive interests, the preconditions for a viable deterrent strategy, the avoidance of trade wars, and stable alliances? The weaving together of a complex argument that appears to be consistent with some real-world process is valuable, just as it is useful to secure qualitative insights into the likely meaning of events and their preconditions. But that is something different from logical consistency. This is not to say that such consistency is always absent from verbal or purely statistical examinations of political events and processes, but it is not their uniform characteristic. It may be true, moreover, that science often advances without first establishing the logical foundations of an idea, but ultimately, those foundations must be established before the word "theory" can be uttered with any meaning and the true value of an insight established. To rank raw conclusions above logical consistency in the overall scheme of what we demand from ourselves as scientists, as Walt does, or to judge the construction of a mathematically precise argument that establishes a sufficient condition for something to be true as less original than the addition of a suggestive, yet vague or incomplete conceptual scheme is not a constructive comparative assessment of alternative intellectual approaches.

The preceding rejoinder, however, gives too much legitimacy to Walt's critique. Consider, for example, the issue of the causes of war. Kenneth Waltz, in *Man, the State, and War*, offers a puzzle, but not one that he solves. Geoffrey Blainey, in *The Causes of War*, helps resolve this puzzle by suggesting that the problem concerns the extent to which, using the game theorist's jargon, the assumption of common knowledge is not satisfied. Finally, Bruce Bueno de Mesquita and David Lalman, in *War and Reason*—one of Walt's whipping boys—dissect Blainey's hypothesis and begin the search for the conditions under which incomplete information rather than common knowledge is the critical parameter in determining the likelihood of conflict. Walt may quibble about their empirical methods, but this sequence of intellectual developments is precisely what any scientist would want to see—paradox, hypothesis, and a logical refinement that clearly differentiates the alternative possibilities. Because understanding requires each step in this process, to judge one step more or less original than the others is nonsense.

Originality in formal analysis does not reside, moreover, in the mere derivation of some result. Given that Walt apparently values models and modeling so little, he cannot see the level of creativity that often goes into a model's design. A precise specification of the problem and the attendant assumptions and constructs do not appear out of thin air. Indeed, the process of model construction (which is often separate from analysis) is much like the informal contemplative processes and freewheeling imagination that Walt so admires. But even this assessment understates the originality of ideas to be found in formal analysis. Consider again the folk theorems of game theory. At first glance, those theorems appear to be mere statements of mathematical logic pertaining to abstract notions of equilibria. Moreover, Walt refers to them as if they were limitations of game theory. We would suggest, however, that barring a demonstration of the reliance of those theorems on constructs and assumptions that other approaches can avoid while treating the same issues, those constructs and assumptions are no more limitations of game theory than they are of any theory. More to the point, however, even if it is true that formal analysts must appeal to such ideas as culture and norms as a way of refining a game-theoretic prediction, we at least have learned the role of such ideas in specific social processes and the theoretical constructs required to study their genesis and evolution.[2] Indeed, it is only the game-theoretic perspective and its attendant formalism that have brought the problems of indeterminacy, coordination, and equilibrium selection to light. And as a consequence, they can now be used to explore such issues as the sources of stability in constitutional design; the possibility that the disagreements over paradigms in international relations concern only an assessment of the likelihood that one equilibrium versus another will be feasible; and, in that context, the functions performed by international organizations, trade, and parallel political structures. If Walt does not see these contributions as original, then his definition of originality must encompass only the generation of incomplete, atheoretical insights.[3]

---

2. See, for example, David K. Lewis, *Convention* (Cambridge: Cambridge University Press, 1969). See also the citations in H. Peyton Young, "The Economics of Convention," *Economic Perspectives*, Vol. 10, No. 2 (Spring 1996), pp. 105–122.
3. See Russell Hardin, "Why a Constitution?" in Bernard Groffman and David Wittman, eds., *The Federalist Papers and the New Institutionalism* (New York: Agathon Press, 1989); and Emerson M.S. Niou and Peter C. Ordeshook, "Less Filling, Tastes Great: The Realist-Neoliberal Debate," *World Politics*, Vol. 46, No. 2 (January 1994), pp. 209–234.

Null Models

Walt stacks the deck against formalism in another way. Much of his discussion is framed by the ostensible purpose of "evaluating the contribution of recent formal work" (p. 8). Any scientific assessment, however, requires a clear and reasoned null hypothesis that is sustained when the evidence fails to support its alternative. In Walt's case, that null appears to be a rather imprecise "inquiry in any other form." Time and again, he tells us of the profound insights gained by other approaches that, we presume, are either inherently beyond the reach or somehow beyond the capacity of formal analysts—profound insights that, if we are to judge by what formal analysis lacks in Walt's view, are "well-verified empirical predictions" (p. 6) that have "been tested in a careful and systematic way" (p. 8). Unfortunately, with the exception of a single footnote citing a few empirical studies of which he approves (see p. 30 n. 72), we are at a loss to learn the identities of those systematically tested hypotheses. Walt cites approvingly Waltz's influential book (p. 17), *Theory of International Politics*, but the editions we see are missing the chapters that offer a critical empirical test of any specific hypothesis. Walt's own *The Origins of Alliances* is an admirable effort at dissecting the processes whereby alliances form and dissolve— one we have found useful in our own research—but eighteen tables (of which nine merely summarize the historical record discussed in the text, four summarize the author's interpretation of specific events, four offer macrodata that can be gleaned from standard sources, and one offers an ad hoc index of "capabilities") hardly qualify as a rigorous empirical test of anything.[4] Walt cites the less formal work of Thomas Schelling, Daniel Ellsberg, and Mancur Olson, although he fails to note the more formal contributions of that age by Kenneth Arrow and Duncan Black or John von Neumann and Oskar Morgenstern's seminal volume, *Theory of Games and Economic Behavior*, upon whose mathematical shoulders all the above stood (though the shoulders upon which Olson stood were those of economists who formalized the preconditions for market failure in the presence of externalities). But with respect to strategic studies, we are unaware of much that meets Walt's demand for systematic testing. Certainly, Walt cannot be referring to the demarcation of ideas among realists, neorealists, liberals, and neoliberals; to any conclusions pertaining to the relative importance of domestic politics; or to insights into the operation of strategic deterrence. And we doubt he is referring to the mainstay "fact"

---

4. Stephen M. Walt, *The Origins of Alliances* (Ithaca, N.Y.: Cornell University Press, 1987).

that democracies never war among themselves, and the dependence of this conclusion on ad hoc operationalizations of the concept of democracy and measures of the severity of conflict.

Walt's failure to contrast clearly the accomplishments of formal analysis with "other approaches" is all the more frustrating because it is true that our less formal intellectual predecessors offer a plethora of valuable insights and ideas that frame the research most students of international affairs, regardless of persuasion, pursue. But in most cases, that research takes the form of attempts to resolve some ambiguity or inconsistency in arguments, for, as we believe any true comparative assessment would show, those predecessors offer a full plate of competing, contradictory, imprecise, and incomplete arguments, hypotheses, and perspectives. It may be true that much of what the formal analyst offers as "substantive conclusion" is well understood or at least consistent with some prior argument (we know colleagues who claim that everything can be found in Aristotle). But showing that a prior conclusion follows logically from some set of initial assumptions is a form of reproducibility that science demands—it tells us that the models in question are not mere fantasy and may not even be fundamentally flawed. Indeed, such redundancy is a form of empirical test that Walt demands to the extent that the initial ideas or conjectures arose from empirical observation. But perhaps more important, we learn something else from the "proof" of an otherwise known conclusion or assertion—we learn the *hidden assumptions* or incomplete logical connections of those earlier arguments, the sufficient conditions for their validity, and, if we are lucky or sufficiently imaginative, their necessary conditions. Indeed, if these assumptions and logical connections were not hidden or incomplete, the prior arguments leading us to them could not have been any less formal than the essays Walt singles out for criticism.

Testing

The fundamental problem with Walt's critique, however, is not the prejudices it reveals or its failure to do what is demanded of the formal analyst—comparative empirical assessment. Rather, it lies in Walt's failure to understand the methods whereby formal and empirical analyses complement each other in any real ongoing scientific enterprise. Walt requires direct empirical application and assessment. Yet the researchers he cites approvingly—Schelling and Olson—as well as Riker, for example, apply formalism differently. Schelling's seminal contribution, *The Strategy of Conflict*, is neither strict formalism nor strict empiricism, but interpretation. He takes a few formal lessons of game theory (e.g., the possibility of multiple equilibria and the importance of sequencing in a game's extensive form) and transforms those ideas into useful applications (to, in the cases cited, the importance of mechanisms of coordination and the nature of viable threats). Olson nowhere offers a test of the theorems about market failure in the presence of externalities upon which his analysis relies (and we are not aware of any prior tests of those theorems in the literature), but by expanding the domain of those rigorously derived results, he opens the door to additional theorizing about substantive matters (e.g., political entrepreneurship and the applied subfield Elinor Ostrom terms "common pool resource" issues).[5] Riker offers perhaps a clearer example of sophisticated "application." Rather than suppose that Arrow's Impossibility Theorem (an exercise in pure deductive formalism) or McKelvey's wholly abstract investigation of the properties of the majority preference relation in generalized spatial preference structures offer results that require direct testing, in *Liberalism against Populism*, Riker uses these ideas to compel a confrontation between two seminormative paradigms of democratic theory, each with extensive policy-relevant implications.[6]

Schelling, Olson, and Riker do not propose to test anything directly, but instead their discussions are skillfully woven and interpreted elements (theorems, structures, and propositions) of formal theory. Walt may lament the small number of such volumes (just as we all do and just as we all should lament the limited number of truly seminal and clear presentations of alternative paradigms in international relations), but we need to understand that the formal essays Walt critiques for having failed to be either sufficiently original or for not offering a direct empirical assessment of their conclusions are only small pieces of a larger puzzle—bricks in an incomplete wall. That the wall is incomplete, however, is merely a call to use those bricks and replicate the talents of Schelling, Olson, and Riker. Riker, in fact, knew only the rudiments of game theory, and barely concerned himself with the proof of such things as McKelvey's instability theorem. But rather than decry the impenetrability of

5. Elinor Ostrom, *Governing the Commons: The Evolution of Institutions for Collective Action* (New York: Cambridge University Press, 1990).
6. William H. Riker, *Liberalism against Populism: A Confrontation between the Theory of Democracy and the Theory of Social Choice* (Prospect Heights, Ill.: Waveland Press, 1982). The essays we cite here as forming the basis of Riker's analysis are Kenneth J. Arrow, *Social Choice and Individual Values* (New Haven, Conn.: Yale University Press, 1951); and Richard D. McKelvey, "General Conditions for Global Intransitivities in Formal Voting Models," *Econometrica*, Vol. 47 (1979), pp. 1085–1112.

that proof (and its reliance on such concepts as continuous and convex preference sets, measurable spaces, upper-semicontinuous functions, etc.), or bemoan the fact that the proof was accompanied by a minimal substantive assessment of its implications or assumptions, Riker succeeds in reshaping our thinking about democratic elections and referendums, the potential for majority tyranny in a democracy, and the strategic options of otherwise disadvantaged political actors. If Walt complains that he cannot find the development of equivalent applications in the formal literature of strategic studies, then one reasonable response is to ask the critic to engage in the interpretive discourse he believes is essential and valuable and set his ideas before us.

The Process of Scientific Development

To comprehend fully our disagreements with Walt, however, it needs to be understood that the development of formal models and their interaction with the empirical world often proceed differently than do the methods of inductive reasoning and "informed opinion." First, by the interchangeable use of words, Walt suffers a confusion between "model" and "theory" when he writes as if they are equivalent. They are not. Theory in our paradigm encompasses a single entity—game theory and its underlying constructs—whereas the research erected on this structure is best described as modeling. It may be true that if models are sufficiently "connected" and if they concern a broad enough range of substantive matters (e.g., microeconomics), then there is little lost in labeling the package "a theory." But nothing approaches this packaging in strategic studies. Of course, a distinction between model and theory does not by itself detract from Walt's core critique—that formal analysis lacks a coherent body of empirically tested or testable propositions. But the distinction does explain that absence as well as the presence of "testing" that Walt deems unsatisfactory. Here let us turn to Walt's discussion of our own work, *The Balance of Power*, which he admittedly treats more kindly than even we might (owing in part to our research subsequent to that effort). Two aspects of our analysis bother Walt. First, he argues that our "empirical analysis ultimately relies on ad hoc factors." Second, he states that "instead of using history to test the model, the model is used to organize the historical narrative" (p. 44). Although we fail to see how this differs from what passes as empirical analysis in strategic studies (or how it differs much from Walt's own research into alliances), we nevertheless take these "criticisms" as compliments. To suppose that a formal model can wholly encompass a complex process that stretches over some forty-five years without resorting to some ad hoc discussion is ludicrous. By definition, that reality must be orders of magnitude more complex than any model, in which case the question becomes: Can the events and patterns we perceive as reality and our understanding of it be organized by anything at all? If a few pages of notation does this in even a modest way—and if, in particular, we can identify those events and patterns that are not yet accommodated by a model and gain a sense of what assumptions are not satisfied in each deviant case—then certainly the analyst has accomplished a great deal.

More specifically, however, it is Walt's first comment that is the more bothersome, for it is here that he reveals his faulty image of empirical scientific research—something akin to researchers scurrying about in white smocks, conducting critical experiments. In fact, most of science consists of the ill-defined and even sometimes random "play" between models, theories, and a complex reality. Rarely does science consist of definitive hypothesis testing, and then only in very restrictive and controlled environments. The reason for this is simple: unless we are concerned with some utterly basic scientific issue, reality is far too complicated to be accommodated in any straightforward way by any simple tractable model. And one implication is that, in general, scientific testing is an imprecise, often informal process. Put simply, productive empirical research, whether in political science or any other field, proceeds differently than what Walt demands of the formal analyst.

The study of politics is, as we argue elsewhere, a field more akin to engineering than to science.[7] Of necessity, our discipline must deal with phenomena that are both too complex for simple, closed-form analysis and too complex for the imprecision of other approaches. This, perhaps, is the attractiveness of imprecision and journalistic discourse—it gives the impression of understanding without revealing the inherent inadequacies of our ideas. But in the natural sciences, we typically learn things about complex systems through an informal, hands-on, trial-and-error process—a process that is informed not merely by careful empirical analysis but also by the failure of models to perform adequately. In trying to solve real-world problems, the natural scientist and engineer often (always?) confront questions they cannot answer theoretically, and the "solution" is an ad hoc "filling in" of the analysis, sometimes using "good guesses" and other times particularistic experiments that Walt

---

7. Peter C. Ordeshook, "Engineering or Science: What Is the Study of Politics?" *Critical Review,* Vol. 9, Nos. 1–2 (Winter–Spring 1995), pp. 175–188.

might term "ad hoc" (e.g., wind tunnels), with the hope that over time and through experience, this filling in will become routinized and even generalized. The practicality of the problems treated, combined with accountability (on the part of the researchers themselves) for faulty judgments, imposes a degree of rigor on this process whereby, as if in some giant bookkeeping enterprise, anomalies and empirical regularities are collected and stored, awaiting theoretical refinement and generalization.

Absent this practical accountability and implicit bookkeeping, much of what passes for "theory testing" in political science is, in fact, the search for empirical regularities that warrant theoretical explanation. But more to the point, this practical interplay is largely absent in political science, and we do not consistently confront the real world in a way that involves sanctions for erroneous advice and predictions. Not much is lost to the rest of the world, or even to the authors themselves, if some argument or conceptual scheme proves worthless or wrong, just as not much is lost to anyone if a student of neorealism, Soviet studies, crisis bargaining, or deterrence theory publishes a volume replete with ambiguity, misconceptions, misperceptions, illogical inferences, or just plain dumb advice. In short, political science lacks the feedback among theory, model, and application that characterizes discovery and empirical assessment in other fields, including even economics. But it is here that logical consistency and rigor gain their greatest advantage for advancing political science as a substantively useful, policy-relevant discipline. Imprecision, vagueness, ambiguity, and the like allow researchers to dodge responsibility behind the shelter of a "reformulation" or "reinterpretation" of their ideas: "The analysis was not wrong, only poorly applied or interpreted." This dodge, however, is far less feasible with rigorous analysis if only because its limitations and failings are, by virtue of its rigor, more readily apparent. And when failure occurs, as it inevitably must, the transparency of formalism allows for the precise cataloging of error, which, of course, is why rigor is valued and why those who eschew it find it uncomfortable.

Finally, we are puzzled most of all by Walt's assertion that "formal rational choice theorists have been largely absent from the major international security debates of the past decade (such as the nature of the post–Cold War world; the character, causes, and strength of the democratic peace; the potential contribution of security institutions; the causes of ethnic conflict; the future role of nuclear weapons; or the impact of ideas and culture on strategy and conflict)" (p. 46). Even if we were to agree with this statement, we would add that the contributions of Walt's "other approaches" to this list of security issues escape us as well. But the list is revealing, for it is the product of someone concerned not with science and empirical regularity as those terms need to be understood for the development of cumulative knowledge, but instead with the commentary and informal discussion we find in newspapers and popular journals that has too long appeared under the label "political *science*." Such discussion and commentary may be entertaining and even sometimes enlightening, but it remains mere journalism until it can be given the solid scientific grounding that formal theorists pursue.

The Modeling Enterprise and Security Studies

Robert Powell

The modeling enterprise is a way of trying to improve our understanding of empirical phenomena. Models serve in this enterprise as a tool for disciplining our thinking about the world, and formal models instill a particular type of discipline. Formalization provides a kind of "accounting standard" that can often help us think through some issues more carefully than ordinary-language arguments can. Just as good accounting standards make a firm's financial situation more transparent to those inside the firm and those outside it, formalization makes arguments more transparent to those making them and to those to whom they are made. When mathematical models are well constructed, they offer us a relatively "clear and precise language for communicating ideas and intuitions."[1]

The contribution that such a standard has to offer to security studies is likely to appear small to those who believe that nonformal or traditional work has already proved its power by amassing a large number of well-established empirical regularities and theoretical explanations of them. By contrast, the benefit of a more transparent standard will seem much higher to those who believe that security studies, like much of international relations theory, has established few robust empirical regularities; to those who have been frustrated to see that almost any outcome can be "explained" after the fact in a way that makes it consistent with existing theories; and to those who have repeatedly tried to formalize many widely held ordinary-language arguments in international relations theory (e.g., anarchy induces a concern for relative gains, anarchy leads to a tendency to balance, and a balance of power is more stable than a preponderance of power), only to find that these arguments are, at best, seriously incomplete and in need of significant qualification.

Robert Powell is Robson Professor of Political Science, University of California, Berkeley, and is the author of Nuclear Deterrence Theory: The Search for Credibility *(Cambridge: Cambridge University Press, 1990) and* In the Shadow of Power *(Princeton, N.J.: Princeton University Press, 1999).*

I am grateful to Bruce Bueno de Mesquita, Elaine Chandler, David Lake, Lisa Martin, James Morrow, and Celeste Wallander for helpful comments or discussion.

1. David Kreps, *Game Theory and Economic Modeling* (New York: Oxford University Press, 1990), p. 6. This book also provides an excellent and accessible overview of some of game theory's contributions and weaknesses.

International Security, Vol. 24, No. 2 (Fall 1999), pp. 97–106

Like most tools, formal models do some things well and others less so.[2] Nevertheless, Stephen Walt denies in "Rigor or Rigor Mortis?" that he is comparing "the relative merits of formal theory with other methodological approaches."[3] I, however, have trouble reading his article any other way. Indeed, a few lines before this denial he seems to say the opposite: "recent formal work has *relatively* little to say about contemporary security issues" (p. 8, emphasis added). And when discussing the originality of the contribution of formal work a few pages later, he also claims, "When *compared* to other research traditions, however, their [formal rational choice theorists'] production of powerful new theories is not very impressive" (p. 22, emphasis added).

My views differ. In the next three sections, I draw on major works taken from nonformal security studies to discuss the issues of reproducibility and transparency (which touch on many of the issues Walt considers under the label "logical consistency"), originality, and empirical evaluation. My purpose is threefold. First, I want to suggest that there are significant foundational problems with many of the most important, widely held arguments in security studies and international relations theory. Even if tightening the connections between assumptions and conclusions were all that formal theory had to offer, this would be a very important contribution at this stage in the development of these fields. After all, these arguments are presumably the intellectual bedrock for more policy-relevant analyses. Second, I believe that when one compares the contribution to security studies of the latest wave of formal theory, which began in the mid-1980s, to that of nonformal theory, the former holds up quite well. Formal theory has made important original contributions, and many formal theories are being tested empirically. Third, I want to show that one can still obtain a badly distorted picture of an entire literature even if one examines only major contributions. No one should judge the rational choice literature on the basis of Walt's summary of eleven examples; nor should anyone judge the overall contribution of mainstream security studies on the basis of the few examples discussed below. One should read the original work with an open mind after attaining some basic background in game theory.[4]

---

2. Paul Krugman, *Development, Geography, and Economic Theory* (Cambridge, Mass.: MIT Press, 1995), offers a thoughtful discussion of the costs and benefits of modeling.
3. Stephen M. Walt, "Rigor or Rigor Mortis? Rational Choice and Security Studies," *International Security*, Vol. 23, No. 4 (Spring 1999), pp. 5–48, at p. 8. Additional references appear parenthetically in the text.
4. Walt worries about the accessibility of game theory, and so do I. But unlike a decade ago, introductory texts are now available to those willing to make a modest investment of time. See,

Finally, a qualification is in order. Walt's article stretches across forty-four pages, whereas I was invited to write a ten-page response. The following discussion will therefore seem abbreviated and perhaps gratuitous at times. To mitigate this, I refer readers at several points to my new book, *In the Shadow of Power*, where I coincidentally address at greater length many of the issues Walt raises.[5]

Reproducibility and Transparency

Reproducibility is an essential element of science. But the importance of reproducibility is not limited to empirical or experimental findings. It also applies to theoretical arguments: if a theoretical argument is given to a group of experts, they should in some sense be able to reproduce it. They should be able to identify the key assumptions and the sequence of steps that lead from those assumptions to the purported conclusions. These experts should also be able to agree if one step follows deductively from previous steps or if it is really an additional assumption.

To be reproducible, arguments need to be transparent. Many ordinary-language arguments in international relations theory lack transparency, however, and this has impeded the development of the field. As an illustration of the lack of transparency and the inability to determine what follows from what and why, consider John Mearsheimer's discussion of realism in "The False Promise of International Institutions."[6] Mearsheimer argues that realism's "pessimistic view of how the world works can be *derived* from realism's five assumptions about the international system" and that "three main patterns of behavior result."[7] The third is that "states aim to maximize their relative power positions over other states."[8] But he then qualifies this derivation in a footnote: "There is disagreement among realists on this point. Some realists argue that states are principally interested in maintaining the existing balance of power, not maximizing relative power."[9]

How is it possible for realists to disagree about a point if it is truly *derived* from realism's basic assumptions? What accounts for these different "deriva-

---

for example, James D. Morrow, *Game Theory for Political Scientists* (Princeton, N.J.: Princeton University Press, 1994).

5. Robert Powell, *In the Shadow of Power* (Princeton, N.J.: Princeton University Press, 1999).
6. John J. Mearsheimer, "The False Promise of International Institutions," *International Security*, Vol. 19, No. 3 (Winter 1994/95), pp. 5–49.
7. Ibid., pp. 10, 11 (emphasis added).
8. Ibid., p. 11.
9. Ibid., n. 27.

tions"? Is it some other (unstated) assumption that, given the importance of the claim, must surely also count as one of realism's basic assumptions? Without a transparent argument, we have no way of knowing.

The ability to determine what follows from realism's basic assumptions is, moreover, terribly important for both theoretical and policy reasons.[10] To test a theory, we need to be able to compare empirical findings with theoretical predictions, and this is impossible if we cannot tell what the theory predicts. Furthermore, policy analyses based on the belief that states "aim to maximize their relative power positions" are likely to be seriously misguided if states actually "are principally interested in maintaining the existing distribution of power" and vice versa.

As a second example of the need for greater transparency, consider Walt's discussion of my "Absolute and Relative Gains in International Relations" and the role that the cost of fighting plays in that analysis.[11] In the simple model I develop in that article, the size of this cost determines whether or not states cooperate. Walt, in turn, claims that this cost is "essentially identical to the concept of the offense-defense balance" (p. 27).[12]

Perhaps so. But one natural formulation of the offense-defense balance is to ask, as Robert Jervis does in his seminal article "Cooperation under the Security Dilemma": "With a given inventory of forces, is it better to attack or to defend?"[13] The larger the difference between the payoffs to attacking and to being attacked, the larger the offensive advantage. Expressing this formally suggests that there may be an important analytic distinction between the overall cost of fighting and the offense-defense *balance*. Suppose there are two states S_1 and S_2 with military inventories m_1 and m_2, respectively. Now take $p_A(m_1, m_2)$ and $p_D(m_1, m_2)$ to be the probabilities that S_1 prevails if it attacks and if it is attacked. Finally, let the payoffs to prevailing and losing be, $1 - c$, and, $- c$, where c is the cost of fighting. Then the expected payoff to attacking is the payoff to winning weighted by the probability of winning plus the payoff to losing times the probability of losing. In symbols, the payoff to attacking is $A = (1 - c) \times p_A(m_1, m_2) + (-c) \times (1 - p_A(m_1, m_2)) = p_A(m_1, m_2) - c$. Similarly,

---

10. See Charles L. Glaser, "Realists as Optimists: Cooperation as Self-Help," *International Security*, Vol. 19, No. 3 (Winter 1994/95), pp. 50–90, for a nonformal effort to trace these consequences. See also Powell, *In the Shadow of Power*, for a more formal effort.

11. Robert Powell, "Absolute and Relative Gains in International Relations," *American Political Science Review*, Vol. 85, No. 4 (December 1991), pp. 1303–1320.

12. Mearsheimer, "The False Promise of International Institutions," p. 22, makes a similar comment.

13. Robert Jervis, "Cooperation under the Security Dilemma," *World Politics*, Vol. 30, No. 2 (January 1978), p. 188.

the payoff to being attacked is $D = p_D(m_1, m_2) - c$. Thus the offense-defense balance (i.e., the difference between the expected payoffs to attacking and to being attacked) is $A - D = p_A(m_1, m_2) - p_D(m_1, m_2)$. This, however, implies that the offense-defense balance does not change if the overall cost of fighting does. Changes in this cost are therefore analytically distinct from the offense-defense balance in this formulation.[14] Whether an increase in this cost and a shift in the offense-defense balance in favor of the latter have similar effects is a conjecture that needs to be investigated theoretically and empirically.[15]

Of course, the empirical effects of a shift in the overall cost of war do not depend on how we define the offense-defense balance and whether or not we incorporate these costs in that definition. Definitions are not given a priori and should be judged by their theoretical usefulness.[16] Walt's inclusion of the cost of fighting in the offense-defense balance suggests that he has a different formulation in mind than the one I have just sketched. But absent a clear specification, it is impossible to tell what that formulation is and what its empirical implications are. Indeed, this is all the more confusing because Walt, like me, cites Jervis's seminal article as the basis for his analysis.

Whether formalization contributes to transparency and reproducibility, and thereby helps further the development of international relations theory, is a pragmatic judgment. Walt and I agree that "formalization is neither necessary nor sufficient for scientific progress" (p. 15). Any formal argument can be translated into ordinary language. One can write out a mathematical equation as an English sentence. Thus any conclusion derived from a formal analysis can in principle be derived from an ordinary-language argument. But, what is possible in principle may not be so in practice. The ordinary-language translations are likely to be long and complicated and difficult to work with.

---

14. If the cost of fighting on the offensive differs from the cost of fighting on the defensive, then the offense-defense balance is $A - D = p_A(m_1, m_2) - p_D(m_1, m_2) - (c_A - c_D)$, where c_A and c_D are the costs of attacking and defending. Again, the offense-defense balance does not change if the overall cost of fighting rises, that is, if c_A and c_D increase by the same amount. Similarly, Charles L. Glaser and Chaim Kaufmann define the offense-defense balance as "the ratio of the cost of the forces that the attacker requires to take territory to the cost of the defender's forces," in "What Is the Offense-Defense Balance and Can We Measure It?" *International Security*, Vol. 22, No. 4 (Spring 1998), p. 46. If, therefore, the costs of fighting on the offensive and defensive rise proportionally, the overall cost increases, but the ratio of these costs and consequently the offense-defense balance, remain constant.
15. Changes in the cost of fighting and the offense-defense balance do have different effects in James D. Fearon, "Bargaining over Objects That Influence Future Bargaining Power," unpublished manuscript, University of Chicago, 1996. See also Powell, *In the Shadow of Power*, for an effort to trace the implications of changes in the cost of fighting and in the offense-defense balance.
16. For a recent discussion of how to define the offense-defense balance, see Glaser and Kaufmann, "What Is the Offense-Defense Balance and Can We Measure It?"

(Indeed, this is the reason for adopting a more formal language.) In practice, recent formal work has produced more transparent and reproducible arguments that show, among other things, that a costly signaling formulation fits the data on deterrence success and failure better than traditional balance-of-interests or balance-of-capabilities arguments do; that the claim that a balance of power is more stable than a preponderance of power needs significant qualification; that the standard argument that anarchy induces a concern for relative gains does not work very well theoretically or empirically; and that the received argument that states generally balance (whether against power or threat) whenever the system is anarchic and populated by units that seek to survive is at best very fragile and often fails to hold.[17]

Originality

Walt conflates two issues in his discussion of originality and formal theory. The first deals with the source of new ideas, and the second is whether work that uses formal models has made a substantial original contribution. As for the first issue, I do not know where deep insights and new ideas come from, and I see no reason to believe that formal theory generally enjoys any "particular advantage as a source of theoretical creativity" (p. 30). The transparency of a model may sometimes spark a new idea for some scholars. But I, like Walt, also believe that "case studies can be an extremely fertile source of new theories" or ideas (p. 31).

The multiplicity of sources of new ideas, however, is not the point. The modeling enterprise is about disciplining our thinking about our ideas regardless of where they come from. Models help forge tighter links between those ideas and their empirical implications, which is an essential step in testing and developing those ideas.

As for the second issue, research, whether formal or not, generally builds on what has come before it. Consequently, judgments about what does and does not constitute an original contribution tend to be subjective. Walt believes that

---

17. For a sampling of formal work on these problems, see James D. Fearon, "Rationalist Explanations of War," *International Organization*, Vol. 49, No. 3 (Summer 1995), pp. 379–414; Fearon, "Signaling versus the Balance of Power and Interests," *Journal of Conflict Resolution*, Vol. 38, No. 2 (June 1994), pp. 236–269; James D. Morrow, "When Do 'Relative Gains' Impede Trade?" *Journal of Conflict Resolution*, Vol. 41, No. 1 (February 1997), pp. 12–37; Robert Powell, "Stability and the Distribution of Power," *World Politics*, Vol. 48, No. 2 (January 1996), pp. 239–267; and Powell, *In the Shadow of Power*.

the formal literature in security studies suffers from a "lack of originality" (p. 23) and briefly summarizes eight examples to try to make his point.

Because of space limitations, I can mention only one. Walt discounts the originality of the work on costly signaling because "the basic idea is virtually identical to Robert Jervis's distinction between 'signals' and 'indices,' which he laid out more than twenty-five years ago" (p. 29) in *The Logic of Images in International Relations*.[18] Jervis's book does make many original contributions. But it seems slightly extreme to suggest that no original work on a subject can be done once a key distinction has been made. After all, John Herz and Herbert Butterfield discussed the basic idea of the security dilemma more than twenty-five years before Jervis's seminal analysis of it.[19]

In "Signaling versus the Balance of Power and Interests," James Fearon differentiates between ex ante and ex post indicators of resolve. An ex ante indicator is a costly signal that is observable before a crisis (e.g., an alliance or foreign assistance), whereas an ex post indicator is a costly signal that is observable only after a crisis begins (e.g., escalation). Both then would seem to be indices in Jervis's terms.[20] The distinction Fearon is making is *not* the same one that Walt attributes to Jervis. Fearon, moreover, goes on to derive specific hypotheses—for example, that ex ante indicators should be positively correlated with general deterrence success but negatively correlated with immediate deterrence success—that actually fit the data better than the received arguments based on the balance of interests or power do. At least by my reading, this contribution is not in *The Logic of Images in International Relations*.[21]

---

18. Robert Jervis, *The Logic of Images in International Relations* (New York: Columbia University Press, 1970).

19. John Herz, "Idealist Internationalism and the Security Dilemma," *World Politics*, Vol. 2, No. 3 (January 1950), pp. 157–180; and Herbert Butterfield, "The Tragic Element in Modern International Conflict," *Review of Politics*, Vol. 12, No. 2 (Winter 1950), pp. 147–164. Arguing, correctly in my view, that Jervis makes a major, original contribution to the security dilemma by linking it to the offense-defense balance is Charles L. Glaser, "The Security Dilemma Revisited," *World Politics*, Vol. 50, No. 1 (October 1997), pp. 171–201.

20. Jervis's discussion of the differences between "signals" and "indices" combines several distinctions that make it difficult to determine if a costly action that a resolute actor would be willing to take but an irresolute actor would be unwilling to take is a "signal" or an "index." For his discussion of these terms see, *The Logic of Images in International Relations*, especially, pp. 18–40.

21. Walt is aware of Fearon's article but treats it oddly. He discusses Fearon's article in the context of logical consistency, where he says that it suggests "*new* ways to interpret a body of *empirical* data," but does not mention this article later when discussing formal theory's originality or its emphasis on empirical validity. See Walt, "Rigor or Rigor Mortis?" p. 15 (emphasis added), for quotation.

Empirical Validity

Walt and I and, as far as I know, all formal modelers agree that the ultimate goal of theory is "to explain real events in the real world" (p. 31). "Mere logical consistency is not sufficient" (p. 32). But Walt and I see different things when we look broadly at the literature. By Walt's count, about 40 percent of the formal articles published in the four major international relations journals between 1989 and 1998 contain systematic empirical tests. He interprets this as evidence that "empirical testing is not a central part of the formal theory enterprise" (p. 33), whereas I see it as evidence of exactly the opposite. Limitations of space prevent me from an extensive discussion of why some formal and nonformal articles may not and, ideally, should not contain systematic empirical tests. Suffice it to say that one reason is that the modeling enterprise often develops through a series of models in which the early models may be very suggestive and insightful but are not tested systematically, just as important ideas in the nonformal literature are often first presented with only brief historical illustrations or a single "plausibility probe."[22]

Walt and I also see different things when we look at specific examples. In my view, Kenneth Waltz's *Theory of International Politics* and Jervis's "Cooperation under the Security Dilemma" are two of the most important and influential pieces published within the last twenty-five years. But neither of these works presents systematic empirical tests of the propositions it develops; nor do they provide a large-N statistical test or offer carefully constructed and executed comparative case studies.

But so what? Systematic empirical testing was not the primary goal of those individual contributions, and I do not infer from its absence that those authors or the literature as a whole is uninterested in systematic empirical evaluation. Similarly I, like Walt, believe that Fearon's "Domestic Political Audiences and the Escalation of International Disputes"[23] "offers an interesting and intuitively plausible conjecture about crisis bargaining, one well worth further exploration" (p. 24). But just as I do not infer from the absence of systematic tests in *Theory of International Politics* or "Cooperation under the Security Dilemma" that Waltz, Jervis, or the nonformal literature as a whole is uninterested in empirical evaluation, I do not infer from the absence of a systematic test in

---

22. See Powell, *In the Shadow of Power*, pp. 23–38, for a discussion of the modeling enterprise.
23. James D. Fearon, "Domestic Political Audiences and the Escalation of International Disputes," *American Political Science Review*, Vol. 88, No. 3 (September 1994), pp. 577–592.

Fearon's article that he or the formal literature as a whole is uninterested in systematic empirical testing.[24] In fact, these ideas are being tested.[25]

Conclusion

I conclude with two points. First, Walt believes that "rational choice theorists have been largely absent from the major international security debates of the past decade (such as the nature of the post–Cold War world; the character, causes, and strength of the democratic peace; the potential contribution of security institutions; the causes of ethnic conflict; the future role of nuclear weapons; and the impact of ideas on strategy and conflict)" (p. 47). I suppose this depends on how one defines "largely absent," but in my view, formal rational choice work is actively contributing to the research on the democratic peace, ethnic conflict, domestic institutional reform, collective security and international institutions, and so on.[26]

Finally, Walt's article and mine are exercises in rhetoric; both exemplify the worst in research design. Walt makes comparative claims about the relative merits of different approaches without presenting systematic comparative evidence, and I carefully select my cases on the dependent variable to counter his

---

24. Indeed, I would find the idea that Fearon's work could in any way be used to exemplify a lack of concern with empirical testing preposterous were that assertion not appearing in the lead article in a major journal.

25. See, for example, Joe Eyerman and Robert Hart, "An Empirical Test of the Audience Cost Proposition," *Journal of Conflict Resolution*, Vol. 40, No. 4 (December 1996), pp. 597–616; Christopher Gelpi and Michael Griesdorf, "Winners or Losers? Democracies in International Crisis, 1918–1988," paper presented at the annual meeting of the American Political Science Association, Washington, D.C., August 28–31, 1997; Gelpi and Joseph Grieco, "Democracy, Crisis Escalation, and the Survival of Political Leaders, 1918–1992," paper presented at the annual meeting of the American Political Science Association, Boston, Massachusetts, September 3–6, 1998; and Kenneth Schultz, "Do Democratic Institutions Constrain or Inform?" *International Organization*, Vol. 53, No. 2 (Spring 1999), pp. 233–266.

26. See, for example, Bruce Bueno de Mesquita and David Lalman, *War and Reason* (New Haven, Conn.: Yale University Press, 1992); Bueno de Mesquita, James D. Morrow, Randoph M. Siverson, and Alastair Smith, "An Institutional Explanation of the Democratic Peace," *American Political Science Review*, Vol. 93, No. 4 (forthcoming, December 1999); George Downs and David Rocke, *Optimal Imperfection?* (Princeton, N.J.: Princeton University Press, 1995); Fearon, "Domestic Audience Costs and the Escalation of International Disputes"; Fearon "Commitment Problems and the Spread of Ethnic Conflict," in David A. Lake and Donald Rothchild, eds., *The International Spread of Ethnic Conflict* (Princeton, N.J.: Princeton University Press, 1998), pp. 107–126; Fearon and David Laitin, "Explaining Interethnic Cooperation," *American Political Science Review*, Vol. 90, No. 4 (December 1994), pp. 715–735; Morrow, "Modeling International Institutions," *International Organization*, Vol. 48, No. 3 (Summer 1994), pp. 387–423; and Schultz, "Do Democratic Institutions Constrain or Inform?"

points.[27] Moreover, neither of us is a disinterested observer; consequently, we tend to see what we want or expect to see, especially because we are not employing any method to help discipline our thinking. No social scientist would take Walt's assessment or mine seriously based on the "evidence" presented. If one wants to assess the relative strengths and weaknesses of the traditional and formal approaches to security studies and international relations theory, one needs to read the work.

27. Walt (p. 8) claims to mitigate this bias by "focusing on some of the best and most widely cited work." But note that I have referred only to some of the best and most widely cited work in nonformal security studies. Observe further that Walt sometimes treats his examples strangely (see, e.g., footnote 21 above).

All Mortis, No Rigor | *Frank C. Zagare*

Like Caesar's view of Gaul, Stephen Walt's evaluation of the recent rational choice literature in strategic studies is divided into three parts.[1] But all the king's horses and all the king's men could not put his article back together again: the analysis of the second section does not follow from the first, and the conclusions of the third cannot be drawn from the second. In the end, Walt's discussion provides a clear illustration of why formal models are so valuable: they provide the strongest possible protection against improper argumentation.

Walt's first section is a reasoned and balanced discussion of the underlying premises of rational choice theory and the rationale for formal modeling. In fact, Walt's summary of the foundations of this methodological technique is refreshing. Unlike many other efforts to evaluate the contributions of game theory to international affairs, it is no caricature.[2] Also uplifting is the absence of vitriol that turned one recent exchange between scholars into an intellectual food fight.[3]

Walt begins by noting the usefulness of mathematical models in ensuring logical consistency, one of three criteria he lists as important for evaluating theories and bodies of literature. Insightfully, he recognizes that the formal literature is not monolithic, that there are important differences among those who use game theory to analyze international politics. As well, Walt's discussion demonstrates a sophisticated understanding of the rationality postulate. Although he does not discuss the issue explicitly, he does not fall into the

Frank C. Zagare is Professor and Chair of the Department of Political Science at the University at Buffalo, State University of New York. He is author of The Dynamics of Deterrence *(Chicago: University of Chicago Press, 1987) and numerous articles applying game theory to international security affairs. He is currently writing a book with D. Marc Kilgour titled* Perfect Deterrence *(New York: Cambridge University Press).*

I wish to thank Bruce Bueno de Mesquita, Erick Duchesne, D. Marc Kilgour, James Morrow, Stephen Quackenbush, William Reed, Paul Senese, and Catherine Zagare for their helpful comments on an earlier draft.

1. Stephen M. Walt, "Rigor or Rigor Mortis? Rational Choice and Security Studies," *International Security*, Vol. 23, No. 4 (Spring 1999), pp. 5–48. All subsequent citations are given by page numbers in the text.
2. See, for example, Martin Hollis and Steve Smith, *Explaining and Understanding International Relations* (Oxford: Clarendon Press, 1990).
3. Specifically, Chalmers Johnson, "Preconception vs. Observation, or the Contributions of Rational Choice Theory and Area Studies to Contemporary Political Science," *PS: Political Science and Politics*, Vol. 30, No. 2 (June 1997), pp. 170–174.

International Security, Vol. 24, No. 2 (Fall 1999), pp. 107–114
© 1999 by the President and Fellows of Harvard College and the Massachusetts Institute of Technology.

common trap of confounding the concept of *instrumental rationality,* which lies at the heart of most applications of game theory, with the theoretically distinct concept of *procedural rationality,* used most frequently by scholars who write in the psychological tradition.[4]

Citing Jon Elster out of context, however, Walt (p. 11) notes that there is *some* disagreement among *some* scholars about the extent to which the rationality assumption is descriptive of actual real-world decisionmaking processes.[5] But Walt seems to gloss over the fact that the vast majority of rational choice theorists, including perhaps all of those whose work he surveys, would agree with Christopher Achen and Duncan Snidal that "the axioms and conclusions of utility theory refer only to choices. Mental calculations are never mentioned: the theory makes no reference to them."[6] In other words, there is almost unanimous agreement among its practitioners that rational choice theory seeks to explain and predict a specific form of human behavior: the choices of real-world decisionmakers. This is one important reason why it is called "choice" theory. Game theory and other theories based on the rationality assumption are not generally viewed as theories of the cognitive process. Walt's (pp. 11–12) suggestion to the contrary is not only beside the point (see below), it is also misleading.

Walt seems to well understand the many virtues of formal methods. Two in particular stand out. Formal models help ensure logical consistency, the sine qua non of good theory, and they enhance clarity by helping to "make the assumptions that drive a conclusion more apparent" (p. 15). Still, he qualifies the significance of these virtues, arguing that originality and empirical accuracy are more important than logical consistency. This is a difficult qualification to accept. Without logical consistency, empirical accuracy cannot be determined, and without empirical accuracy, originality is of little moment, as Walt rightfully notes (p. 13).

At this point, we detect the first hint why Walt is so tolerant of logical inconsistency. Being able to argue both ways is a valuable rhetorical skill. For example, he praises Kenneth Waltz's *Theory of International Politics* for its

---

4. Frank C. Zagare, "Rationality and Deterrence," *World Politics,* Vol. 42, No. 2 (January 1990), pp. 238–260.

5. After noting what would constitute an "ideal" rational choice explanation, Elster also goes on to say that "scrutinizing mental states to ensure satisfaction of the causal conditions is then both impossible and pointless." See his "Introduction," in Jon Elster, ed., *Rational Choice* (New York: New York University Press, 1986), p. 16.

6. Christopher H. Achen and Duncan Snidal, "Rational Deterrence Theory and Comparative Case Studies," *World Politics,* Vol. 41, No. 2 (January 1989), p. 164.

originality, excusing its contradictions.[7] But if Walt were to use the same definition of originality that he applies to the formal models he later surveys (see pp. 26–31), Waltz's nuanced reformulation of balance-of-power theory would not pass the test. Indeed, the attractiveness of Waltz's (informal) deductive model lies in the transparency and strength of its logic, and in Waltz's stubborn refusal to abandon that logic to reach logically inconsistent policy conclusions. More specifically, one important reason that Waltz's theoretical work is much to be admired is that it demonstrates a logical connection between his assumption that states are security maximizers, his predictions about balancing and the stability of bipolar systems, and his prescription that favors the selective proliferation of nuclear weapons. But neither the argument that nuclear parity relationships are exceedingly stable, the claim that states tend to balance, nor the recommendation that nuclear technology ought to be shared is original to Waltz.

Walt next seems to forget his earlier observation that there is a controversy among some theorists "over whether rational choice theories must merely be consistent with the observed outcome, or whether they must also be consistent with the actual process by which decisions are made" (p. 11). Speaking about the descriptive accuracy of Bayes's rule, he takes the extreme (minority) view, asserting that "if human decisions in the real world are not made in the way that rational choice theorists assume . . . then the models may be both deductively consistent and empirically wrong" (p. 17). Some rational choice theories may indeed be empirically inaccurate and, therefore, rightfully ignored or discarded, but the fact that decisionmakers do not consciously use Bayes's rule to update their prior beliefs after new information is acquired is beside the point, as the quote from Achen and Snidal should make clear.

For one thing, it would be a simple matter to substitute other updating rules. In this case, Walt's point evaporates. The strengths of formal models are not tied to any particular assumption about the way beliefs are updated in the light of new evidence. For another, assumptions are extremely useful simplifying devices. They would, in fact, lose their utility if they were completely accurate descriptions of real-world processes. In other words, theories should be judged by their logical consistency and empirical accuracy, not by the descriptive validity of their assumptions. Assumptions should be judged by their ability to generate empirically correct propositions. *If* Bayes's rule is problematic

---

7. Kenneth N. Waltz, *Theory of International Politics* (Reading, Mass.: Addison-Wesley, 1979).

because it leads to empirically inaccurate statements, it could and should be eliminated.[8]

Finally, Walt changes course and contradicts himself, once again, by asserting that "formal methods . . . make it easier to bury key assumptions within the model" (p. 20). Walt's complaint seems to be motivated by the "time and effort [needed] to unearth the basic logic of the argument." For Walt, this is regrettable because "the time required to understand an elaborate formal demonstration . . . is time that cannot be spent questioning underlying assumptions or testing the empirical validity of the argument" (pp. 21–22). But what better way is there to evaluate assumptions than by exploring their logical consequences, and what better way is there to judge an empirical generalization's standing than by evaluating the logic that can explain it?

Consider now the third conceptually distinct section of Walt's article, which contains his main conclusion: the field of "security studies should welcome contributions from formal theory, large-*N* statistical analysis, historical case studies, and even the more rigorous forms of interpretive or constructivist analysis" (p. 48). It is hard to find fault here. Tolerance, intellectual or otherwise, is an important virtue. Without it, intellectual fields would calcify: new ideas would not surface, and scientific progress would come to a dead halt.

Walt's conclusions are admirable, but they are not supported by his literature review. To show this, I next assess the merits of the arguments and criticisms Walt makes in the second section of his article. My purpose in doing so, however, is not to undermine his plea for intellectual toleration. Rather, it is to highlight inconsistencies and inaccuracies in his argument. After all, the accurate representation of ideas is another important scholarly virtue. It is simply not necessary to accept Walt's characterization of the rational choice literature in order to be sympathetic with his main conclusion.

Given that others will no doubt focus on Walt's understanding of their research, I begin with his characterization of my work with D. Marc Kilgour. It is interesting to observe at the outset that Walt discusses only one of a number of articles that Kilgour and I have coauthored, and an article that was published in 1991 at that. Since then, we have extended the basic mutual deterrence model that Walt offers as a leading example of "methodological overkill" to analyze unilateral (or asymmetric) deterrence relationships in which there is both a challenger and a defender of the status quo; we have refined the core unilateral deterrence model to explore the dynamics of the

---

8. Parenthetically, Walt misstates the so-called folk theorem, which holds that in an infinitely repeated *n*-person game any combination of action choices that is individually rational can be part of some equilibrium.

escalation process and to evaluate competing extended deterrence deployment policies such as massive retaliation and flexible response; we have used the extended deterrence model to delve into the conditions associated with limited conflicts and escalation spirals; and we have applied the underlying model to determine the role played by a client state in determining the success or failure of extended deterrence.[9]

Because we stand by most of what we said in the article in question, it would be very easy to overlook the selective treatment of our work, except that, in another forum, Walt complained about the "small sample size" of John Vasquez's evaluation of classical realism in general and of Walt's work in particular.[10] No wonder, then, that Walt does not place the highest value on logical consistency. Logical consistency would not allow Walt to use one standard by which to denigrate Vasquez's assessment of his own work, and then to ignore that standard in evaluating the work of others.

Walt claims that the conclusions of our model are "for the most part affirmations of the conventional wisdom" (p. 23), asserting that "Kilgour and Zagare have reinvented the central elements of deterrence theory without improving on it" (p. 24). I will not comment on whether or not our argumentation is an improvement on classical deterrence theory. That is for others to judge. But Walt's claim that our argument is merely a restatement of classical deterrence theory is clearly inaccurate.

Our theory is drawn from an entirely different axiomatic base than is classical deterrence theory. Classical deterrence theory starts with the assumption that war in the nuclear age is irrational, which is simply another way of saying that all endgame threats are inherently incredible. As well, game-theoretic models in the classical tradition generally assume that all attack choices result in war.[11] By contrast, in the theory that Kilgour and I have developed—we

---

9. See, in particular, Frank C. Zagare and D. Marc Kilgour, "Asymmetric Deterrence," *International Studies Quarterly*, Vol. 37, No. 1 (March 1993), pp. 1–27; Zagare and Kilgour, "Modeling 'Massive Retaliation,'" *Conflict Management and Peace Science*, Vol. 13, No. 1 (Fall 1993), pp. 61–86; Zagare and Kilgour, "Assessing Competing Defense Postures: The Strategic Implications of 'Flexible Response,'" *World Politics*, Vol. 47, No. 3 (April 1995), pp. 373–417; Zagare and Kilgour, "Deterrence Theory and the Spiral Model Revisited," *Journal of Theoretical Politics*, Vol. 10, No. 1 (January 1998), pp. 59–87; Kilgour and Zagare, "Uncertainty and the Role of the Pawn in Extended Deterrence," *Synthese*, Vol. 100, No. 3 (September 1994), pp. 379–412; and Zagare and Kilgour, *Perfect Deterrence* (New York: Cambridge Univerisity Press, forthcoming).
10. Stephen M. Walt, "The Progressive Power of Realism," *American Political Science Review*, Vol. 91, No. 4 (December 1997), p. 934; and John A. Vasquez, "The Realist Paradigm and Degenerative versus Progressive Research Programs: An Appraisal of Neotraditional Research on Waltz's Balancing Proposition," ibid., pp. 899–912.
11. For a discussion, see Frank C. Zagare, "Classical Deterrence Theory: A Critical Assessment," *International Interactions*, Vol. 21, No. 4 (1996), pp. 365–387; Zagare, "Rationality and Deterrence," pp. 251–257; and Zagare and Kilgour, *Perfect Deterrence*.

now call it "perfect deterrence theory"—threat credibility is a variable. Moreover, in the family of interrelated deterrence models we have developed, states are afforded an opportunity not to respond to an outright attack. These are small but critical differences.

Given the above, it should not be surprising to learn that many (but not all) of our conclusions are at odds with more standard formulations. For example, contrary to those classical deterrence theorists who support an "overkill" capability, perfect deterrence theory suggests that a "minimum deterrent" capability is better. Perfect deterrence theory also suggests that, during a crisis, reciprocating rather than preemptive strategies should be adopted. This prescription clearly runs counter to the implications of the work of Thomas Schelling, Daniel Ellsberg, and Robert Powell.[12] And finally, contrary to arguments made by Waltz, Bruce Bueno de Mesquita and William Riker, and several others, perfect deterrence theory concludes that proliferation policies are dangerous and should be eschewed.[13] In short, perfect deterrence theory seeks to refine and improve classical deterrence theory, much the way Waltz's theory seeks to refine and improve classical balance-of-power theory.

Perhaps it is an inconsequential fact that Walt has misrepresented our work, committing in the process the very same sin he himself railed against in "The Progressive Power of Realism." Still, it is interesting to observe that Walt at once suggests that the implications of our model are "not very illuminating" (p. 24) and that James Morrow's crisis bargaining model yields "rather trivial results" (p. 23).[14] Yet he also claims that "Kilgour and Zagare's model produces results different from Morrow's model" (p. 25 n. 51). For the sake of argument, I am prepared to accept Walt's evaluation of our model's implications, but then Morrow's model cannot also be said to be theoretically trivial. Again, it is not surprising that Walt is willing to tolerate logical inconsistency. It allows him to assert that two models with divergent implications both produce obvious

12. Thomas C. Schelling, *The Strategy of Conflict* (Cambridge, Mass.: Harvard University Press, 1960); Schelling, *Arms and Influence* (New Haven, Conn.: Yale University Press, 1966); and Daniel Ellsberg, "The Theory and Practice of Blackmail," lecture at the Lowell Institute, Boston, Massachusetts, March 10, 1959, reprinted in Oran R. Young, ed., *Bargaining: Formal Theories of Negotiation* (Urbana: University of Illinois Press, 1975). See also Robert Powell, *Nuclear Deterrence Theory: The Search for Credibility* (New York: Cambridge University Press, 1990).
13. Kenneth N. Waltz, "The Spread of Nuclear Weapons: More May Be Better," Adelphi Paper No. 171 (London: International Institute for Strategic Studies, 1981); and Bruce Bueno de Mesquita and William H. Riker, "An Assessment of the Merits of Selective Nuclear Proliferation," *Journal of Conflict Resolution*, Vol. 26, No. 2 (June 1982), pp. 283–306.
14. James D. Morrow, "Capabilities, Uncertainty, and Resolve: A Limited Information Model of Crisis Bargaining," *American Journal of Political Science*, Vol. 33, No. 4 (November 1980), pp. 941–972.

conclusions. Like former New York Yankees manager Billy Martin, Walt apparently feels strongly both ways.

The larger issue, however, is whether a formal model that produces conclusions that may have been stated elsewhere is still to be valued as having made a contribution to international relations theory. Unless Walt is ready to deny the importance of rigorous argumentation, the answer must be in the affirmative. Conclusions, empirical or otherwise, devoid of logical argumentation are of little value. Opinions about national security policies are a dime a dozen. They acquire currency only when they are supported by a logical structure. In this sense, a formal argument adds value, even to widely accepted conclusions.

But the contributions of rigorous analysis go much further than this. Suppose that two logical structures support diametrically opposite positions, as do Bueno de Mesquita and Riker's deterrence model, which supports selected proliferation policies, and the corpus of Zagare and Kilgour, which supports the opposite conclusion. Unlike loosely stated arguments that favor or oppose a particular policy, the logical structure of the underlying formal models can easily be counterposed, revealing the assumptions that give rise to the differences.

I shall not continue to rehearse the many additional benefits of formal models. As mentioned, Walt does a good job of this, even though, Janus-like, he felt compelled to abandon his even-handed analysis with a desultory review of prominent examples of applications of formal work in international security. Nonetheless, it is difficult to pass over the opportunity to highlight one final inconsistency. Walt (correctly) points out that most formal theorists have not devoted themselves to rigorous empirical validation of their models, although there have been attempts to use game-theoretic models to analyze particular crises and critical strategic relationships that he overlooks (for reasons I shall not speculate on).[15] But at least two points should be emphasized here. First, those who do large-N quantitative research do not regard Walt's own work as systematically empirical, so it is odd that he would find fault with formal theorists on this count.[16] Second, and more important, the lack of systematic

---

15. See, for instance, Frank C. Zagare, *The Dynamics of Deterrence* (Chicago: University of Chicago Press, 1987).
16. See, for example, Randolph M. Siverson's review of Walt's *The Origins of Alliances* in the *American Political Science Review*, Vol. 82, No. 3 (September 1988), pp. 1044–1045. This may be an unfair criticism if Walt does not mean to imply that formal modelers should subject their work to large-N statistical tests. But then why does he ignore those studies that apply game theory to real-world situations? See, for example, Frank C. Zagare, "A Game-Theoretic Analysis of the Vietnam Negotiations: Preferences and Strategies 1968–1973," *Journal of Conflict Resolution*, Vol. 21,

empirical research by formal theorists has more to do with the division of labor in the discipline than it does with any innate limitations of formal (or even informal) theory. Thus Walt's observation, even if accepted, is largely irrelevant. In other words, careful empirical research is not precluded by the tenets of the paradigm.

To conclude, I readily accept Walt's call for intellectual tolerance and, indeed, applaud it. Nonetheless, I reject his point of view that logical inconsistency is a price that must be paid for scientific advancement. There can be no compromise here. Without a logically consistent theoretical structure to explain them, empirical observations are impossible to evaluate; without a logically consistent theoretical structure to constrain them, original and creative theories are of limited utility; and without a logically consistent argument to support them, even entirely laudable conclusions, such as Walt's, lose much of their intellectual force.

No. 4 (December 1977), pp. 663–684; Zagare, "The Geneva Conference of 1954: A Case of Tacit Deception," *International Studies Quarterly*, Vol. 23, No. 3 (September 1979), pp. 390–411; Zagare, "Nonmyopic Equilibria and the Middle East Crisis of 1967," *Conflict Management and Peace Science*, Vol. 5, No. 2 (Spring 1981), pp. 139–162; and Zagare, "A Game-Theoretical Evaluation of the Cease-Fire Alert Decision of 1973," *Journal of Peace Research*, Vol. 20, No. 1 (April 1983), pp. 73–86.

A Model Disagreement | *Stephen M. Walt*

$\mathbf{M}$y purpose in writing "Rigor or Rigor Mortis?" was to evaluate the contributions of formal rational choice theory to the field of security studies.[1] I argued that formal theory was useful—but not essential—for developing precise and logically sound arguments, and suggested that the benefits of formalization were not cost-free. I also argued that recent formal work had not produced a significant body of new and original insights, and I sought to show that much of this work was either untested or empirically questionable. Accordingly, I concluded that although formal theory could be a valuable part of the field, it was not intrinsically superior to other well-established research techniques. As a result, I emphasized that the field of security studies should strive to maintain its methodological pluralism. To paraphrase Georges Clemenceau, the study of warfare is too important to be left solely to formal modelers.

The five responses to my article raise many important issues. Lacking sufficient space to address all of them, I focus here on the central points that divide us. I do not believe that the responses cast serious doubt on my original claims, and as I attempt to show below, several of them actually provide additional support for my position.

My reply consists of five sections. The first section considers the issue of logical consistency and precision, which several of the respondents declare to be the most important feature of a scientific theory and the cardinal virtue of formal techniques. The second section examines the question of creativity and originality and shows why the examples of innovative work offered by my critics do not undermine my original assessment. The third section revisits the issue of empirical validity and shows that the responses actually lend further support to my central argument. The fourth section addresses the crucial issue of policy relevance, which is still a major liability of formal work in the field of security studies. The fifth section considers the hegemonic aspirations of the modeling community and reiterates my plea for methodological pluralism.

Stephen M. Walt is the Evron M. and Jeane J. Kirkpatrick Professor of International Affairs at the John F. Kennedy School of Government, Harvard University.

1. Stephen M. Walt, "Rigor or Rigor Mortis? Rational Choice and Security Studies," *International Security*, Vol. 23, No. 4 (Spring 1999), pp. 5–48. Further references appear parenthetically in the text.

International Security, Vol. 24, No. 2 (Fall 1999), pp. 115–130

Logical Consistency and Precision

The responses to my article make two main claims on the subject of logical consistency and precision. The first claim is that I place little value on this criterion, thereby stacking the deck against formal modeling.[2] The second claim is that logical consistency is the sine qua non of any scientific theory, a claim intended to demonstrate the intrinsic superiority of formal techniques. The first charge is false; the second merits additional discussion.

Contrary to the first assertion, I do not denigrate logical consistency or precision. As I wrote in my article, social science "requires theories that are logically consistent, precise, original, and empirically valid." I also declared that "other things being equal, theories that are stated precisely and that are internally consistent are preferable to theories that are vague or partly contradictory," adding that "logical consistency is highly desirable and efforts to achieve it are a central aim of science." And I went to some lengths to point out that this was an area where formalization could make a contribution (pp. 8, 12, 17). Like motherhood and apple pie, in short, logical consistency is something that all of us endorse.

Where we differ is in the relative importance of this criterion and the relative performance of formal and nonformal approaches. Several respondents assert that logical consistency is the most important criterion for judging a social science theory. This view is clearest in the response by Bruce Bueno de Mesquita and James Morrow, who write that "logical consistency takes precedence over [creativity and empirical validity]," adding that it enjoys "pride of place among the criteria for judging social science theories."[3] I disagree. Although consistency and precision are valuable, they are not the only—or even the most important—qualities that scientists look for in a theory. And as I noted in my article, formalization is neither necessary to achieve consistency nor sufficient to guarantee useful results.

First, logical consistency alone is essentially meaningless, for one can derive any conclusion one wishes if one begins with the right set of premises. It is not surprising, for example, that formal theorists often reach logically consistent but contrary conclusions, and logic alone cannot tell us which one is

---

2. See Lisa L. Martin, "The Contributions of Rational Choice: A Defense of Pluralism," p. 82 n. 10; Emerson M.S. Niou and Peter C. Ordeshook, "Return of the Luddites," pp. 85–86; and Frank C. Zagare, "All Mortis, No Rigor," p. 108, all in *International Security*, Vol. 24, No. 2 (Fall 1999).
3. Bruce Bueno de Mesquita and James D. Morrow, "Sorting Through the Wealth of Notions," pp. 56–57, ibid.

correct.[4] For this reason, Einstein declared that "even the most lucidly logical mathematical theory was of itself no guarantee of truth."[5]

Second, I stand by my claim that "although all three criteria are important. . . . originality and empirical validity are especially prized" (p. 13). Bold new theories understandably attract greater attention than subsequent efforts to tidy up the fine details of an argument. A creative new theory is unlikely to last long if it is wholly contradictory, but it will deserve widespread attention even if it rests on as-yet unidentified assumptions or contains causal claims that have to be qualified upon closer inspection. Why? Because a powerful new argument can be useful even when it contains inconsistencies, and because refining the logic of an argument is easier once one has an argument to examine.[6] Both creating a new theory and refining its logic are useful parts of science, but the first one gets the loudest applause.

Third, formalization is not necessary to make precise, logically consistent arguments.[7] Although critics like Emerson Niou and Peter Ordeshook regard virtually all nonformal work in social science as "mired in imprecision, vagueness, obscure logic, ill-defined constructs, nontestable hypotheses, and ad hoc argument," I believe many nonformal works of social science are clear, logical, and precise.[8] Moreover, the underlying logic of many nonformal works is frequently easier to discern than an elaborate formal model, even for those who have acquainted themselves with the latter method.[9]

---

4. Compare, for example, Frank C. Zagare and D. Marc Kilgour, *Perfect Deterrence* (New York: Cambridge University Press, forthcoming); and Bruce Bueno de Mesquita and William Riker, "An Assessment of the Merits of Selective Nuclear Proliferation," *Journal of Conflict Resolution* Vol. 26, No. 2 (June 1982), pp. 283–306; or Robert Powell, "Stability and the Distribution of Power," *World Politics*, Vol. 48, No. 2 (January 1996), pp. 239–267; Bueno de Mesquita and David Lalman, *War and Reason: Domestic and International Imperatives* (New Haven, Conn.: Yale University Press, 1992), pp. 190, 205–206; and James D. Fearon, "War, Relative Power, and Private Information," paper presented at the annual meeting of the International Studies Association, Atlanta, Georgia, March 31–April 4, 1992.

5. Albert Einstein, quoted in Timothy Ferris, *The Whole Shebang: A State of the Universe(s) Report* (New York: Touchstone, 1997), p. 28.

6. This is true even of the most basic research tools. The calculus was a research tool of enormous value from the moment it was invented, but "a century and a half elapsed between the time the calculus was invented and the time [Augustin-Louis] Cauchy successfully gave it a logically acceptable form." See Judith V. Grabiner, *The Origins of Cauchy's Rigorous Calculus* (Cambridge, Mass.: MIT Press, 1981), p. 16.

7. It should be noted that Bueno de Mesquita and Morrow and Martin acknowledge this point. See Bueno de Mesquita and Morrow, "Sorting Through the Wealth of Notions," p. 58; and Martin, "Contributions of Rational Choice," p. 76.

8. Niou and Ordeshook, "Return of the Luddites," p. 87.

9. Robert Powell argues that nonformal theories suffer from a "lack of transparency" and an "inability to determine what follows from what," citing as evidence the fact that realists like John Mearsheimer and Charles Glaser disagree about certain aspects of international politics. See

Fourth, much of the recent formal work in security studies does not devote a great deal of effort to identifying and resolving the (alleged) inconsistencies of nonformal scholarship. Rather, in many cases models are used to identify underlying assumptions or boundary conditions (i.e., the conditions that must obtain if an existing hypothesis is expected to operate). As I noted in my article, this sort of analysis can be useful. But identifying underlying assumptions or boundary conditions is not the same as showing that a well-verified non-formal theory was internally contradictory. And given the importance that my critics place on this criterion, it is noteworthy that they offer at most a single example of a logically contradictory argument that was corrected through formal analysis.[10]

Are Formal Modelers Creative?

All of the responses suggest that I underestimated the originality of recent formal work. Niou and Ordeshook emphasize the creativity that modeling requires, and several respondents suggest that I neglected important recent works or mischaracterized the works I did discuss. Both Lisa Martin and Frank Zagare also argue that it is unfair to focus on individual works rather than an entire stream of interrelated models. I consider each of these assertions in turn.

First, Niou and Ordeshook argue that I "cannot see the level of creativity that often goes into a model's design," noting also that "logical consistency is itself a profoundly important creative contribution."[11] The issue, however, is not whether the construction of a model involves creative thought; rather, it is whether the model leads to new, empirically valid insights about international security. As described in my article, this is usually not the case.

Second, Bueno de Mesquita and Morrow and Robert Powell challenge my assessment of a number of recent formal works, and offer a seemingly daunting list of "original contributions" made by formal modelers. Space does not permit me to discuss every one of the works they invoke (some of which are

Powell, "The Modeling Enterprise and Security Studies," *International Security*, Vol. 24, No. 2 (Fall 1999), pp. 99–100. In fact, it is quite easy to identify why scholars in the realist tradition reach different conclusions; see Stephen Brooks, "Dueling Realisms," *International Organization*, Vol. 51, No. 4 (Summer 1997), pp. 445–477.

10. Martin points out that Thomas Schelling made somewhat inconsistent statements in two separate books, published six years apart. See Martin, "The Contributions of Rational Choice," p. 79.

11. See Niou and Ordeshook, "Return of the Luddites," pp. 88, 89. Note the priority attached to logical consistency here as well.

still awaiting publication as of this writing), but a brief discussion will show that their list is not as compelling as it might appear.

COUNTEREXAMPLE NO. 1. Robert Powell, "Crisis Stability in the Nuclear Age."[12] This article suggests that Thomas Schelling's famous argument about the reciprocal fear of surprise attack depended on a hidden assumption (i.e., that neither side had the option of simply surrendering the stakes). I would make two points in response. First, this is an example of formal theory being used to identify boundary conditions rather than to make a new and original hypothesis. Second, Powell's argument amounts to saying that first-strike advantages do not make war inevitable so long as either side can avoid war by surrendering. This may be a useful qualification to Schelling, but it is hardly a surprising claim.

COUNTEREXAMPLE NO. 2. James D. Morrow, "Allies and Asymmetry: An Alternative to the Capability Aggregation Model of Alliances."[13] Bueno de Mesquita and Morrow argue that this article shows why states sometimes form alliances for reasons other than security. The article does not contain a formal model, however, and the central point—that alliances may involve one state sacrificing autonomy for security while its partners gain autonomy by providing it with greater security—does not require a formal presentation. As such, it cannot be invoked to demonstrate the fertility of formal techniques.

COUNTEREXAMPLE NO. 3. Randall Calvert, "The Value of Biased Information."[14] Contrary to Bueno de Mesquita and Morrow's claim, this article does not show that "it is rational for political leaders to surround themselves with 'yes-men.'"[15] Rather, Calvert presents a highly stylized model in which leaders "rationally" place greater weight on advice from those whose views they share than from those they regard as dissenters. The article does not "show" that political leaders *should* surround themselves with yes-men, however, because such a policy can create other dangers (such as a failure to consider a full range of alternatives) that exceed the benefits implied by the model. Calvert's article presents no empirical evidence, and it is worth noting that Alexander George's original work on multiple advocacy (which they portray as contrary to Cal-

---

12. Robert Powell, "Crisis Stability in the Nuclear Age," *American Political Science Review*, Vol. 83, No. 1 (March 1989), pp. 61–76.
13. James D. Morrow," "Allies and Asymmetry: An Alternative to the Capability Aggregation Model of Alliances," *American Journal of Political Science*, Vol. 35, No. 4 (November 1991), pp. 904–933.
14. Randall Calvert, "The Value of Biased Information," *Journal of Politics*, Vol. 47, No. 3 (May 1985), pp. 530–555.
15. Bueno de Mesquita and Morrow, "Sorting Through the Wealth of Notions," p. 62.

vert's model) explicitly warned that the views of those known to be dissenters may be discounted in the policymaking process.[16]

COUNTEREXAMPLE NO. 4. James D. Morrow, "Electoral Incentives and Arms Control."[17] This article presents and tests a formal model linking domestic political considerations to negotiating positions on strategic arms control. The basic argument is that U.S. leaders will make more concessions as economic conditions worsen, but only up to a so-called turnover point. The model is largely atheoretical (i.e., the purported links between economic conditions, congressional preferences, and Soviet and U.S. negotiating positions are not well specified), and Morrow concedes that the evidence for his model is not very strong. He describes the statistical results as "suggestive," but admits that "they do not constitute conclusive evidence." He also acknowledges that "key [congressional] votes in future quarters produce mixed results depending on the exact specification." Although he runs a variety of regressions searching for the best fit, many of the regression coefficients do not achieve statistical significance. Thus Morrow concludes that "given the weakness of the statistical results, the question of whether turnover points exist remains open."[18] This article provides evidence of Morrow's honesty (he admits that the model is not well supported), but it is hardly a good example of new and original insights resulting from formal theory.

COUNTEREXAMPLE NO. 5. Joanne Gowa, "Bipolarity, Multipolarity, and Free Trade."[19] Gowa's article argues that the desire to strengthen one's allies can encourage great powers in a bipolar world to adopt policies of free trade. The central point to note, however, is that Gowa's article is not an example of formal theory. She does employ simple 2 × 2 games to illustrate her argument (including the familiar prisoners' dilemma), but she derives no equilibria and does not deduce testable hypotheses from the formal structure. Interestingly, Bueno de Mesquita and Morrow do not claim that formal theory led to

---

16. George cites George Ball's opposition to President Lyndon Johnson's Vietnam policies as a case where a dissenter's advice was discounted because he "did not share the top policy makers' premise that Vietnam had become strategically important to the United States." See Alexander L. George, "The Case for Multiple Advocacy in Making Foreign Policy," *American Political Science Review*, Vol. 66, No. 3 (September 1972), p. 773.

17. James D. Morrow, "Electoral Incentives and Arms Control," *Journal of Conflict Resolution*, Vol. 35, No. 2 (June 1991), pp. 243–265.

18. Ibid., pp. 261, 262, 265.

19. Joanne Gowa, "Bipolarity, Multipolarity, and Free Trade," *American Political Science Review*, Vol. 83, No. 4 (December 1989), pp. 1245–1256.

powerful new insights in this case. Rather, they merely assert that "the formal nature of Gowa's argument *facilitated* this theoretically fruitful debate."[20]

COUNTEREXAMPLE NO. 6. James D. Fearon, "Rationalist Explanations for War."[21] Bueno de Mesquita and Morrow argue that I mischaracterize Fearon's arguments about the effects of anarchy and private information. I disagree. Standard treatments of anarchy do not deny that states can reach agreements (and even abide by them): the main point is that the commitment problem has long been understood to be a central feature of anarchy. Similarly, I did not argue that there was no difference between "secrecy" and "private information," only that both can foster miscalculation and lead to war via essentially the same mechanism. Furthermore, although some forms of secrecy can be revealed in order to facilitate a deal, opponents are unlikely to take an enemy's revelations at face value. Thus the distinction between "secrecy" and "private information" may be difficult to discern in practice. Finally, my point was not that Fearon's article made no contribution at all, only that its central theoretical claims were not new.

COUNTEREXAMPLE NO. 7. Woosang Kim and James D. Morrow, "When Do Power Shifts Lead to War?"[22] Bueno de Mesquita and Morrow argue that this article yields a number of novel insights. What "novel hypotheses" does it offer? First, "risk-acceptant rising states and risk-averse declining states increase the chance of war." Second, "the greater the rising state's dissatisfaction with the status quo, the more likely war is." Third, "the lower the expected costs of war, the more likely war is." These propositions are obvious, and the second and third are almost tautological. The fourth hypothesis—"war is more likely when the parties are roughly but not exactly equal in capabilities"—is less obvious, but hardly new.[23] Kim and Morrow perform a number of statistical tests of these propositions, and the results provide only partial support for their conjectures. (Among other things, the results are quite sensitive to the specific measures used to estimate the variables in the model.) Thus it is not clear how much has been learned from formalizing the problem as they do.

COUNTEREXAMPLE NO. 8. In his response, Powell challenges my assessment of recent formal work by observing that there are subtle differences between

---

20. Bueno de Mesquita and Morrow, "Sorting Through the Wealth of Notions," p. 64 (emphasis added).

21. James D. Fearon, "Rationalist Explanations for War," *International Organization*, Vol. 49, No. 3 (Summer 1995), pp. 379–414.

22. Woosang Kim and James D. Morrow, "When Do Power Shifts Lead to War?" *American Journal of Political Science*, Vol. 36, No. 4 (November 1992), pp. 896–922.

23. Ibid., p. 907.

certain recent formal treatments and the work of earlier scholars (e.g., Robert Jervis). In particular, he argues that his definition of the "costs of war" differs from Jervis's depiction of the "offense-defense balance."[24]

I agree that Powell's formulation of the costs of war in his article on relative gains is "analytically distinct" from *some* of the ways that the offense-defense balance has been defined in the literature. But the central *theoretical* argument advanced is not new: when military technology, geography, and so on make warfare more profitable, states will be more fearful of one another and less inclined to cooperate. Reasonable people can disagree over whether this is a major breakthrough or merely a simple refinement, but it is worth noting that Powell himself regards Jervis's article as the "seminal" analysis underpinning his own claim.

Finally, both Martin and Zagare suggest that it is unfair to examine individual articles in isolation, because a cardinal virtue of modeling is the capacity "to generate linked, coherent sets of propositions and insights."[25] Maybe so, but they offer no examples of where this capacity led to new and original ideas. Moreover, because any theory rests on a potentially infinite number of assumptions, one can always generate a new model by altering a key assumption of an earlier model, thereby generating a stream of interrelated models and creating the appearance of scholarly momentum.[26] Unless some effort is made to summarize and test the potentially infinite number of competing models, however, it is not clear what the overall contribution is. And as Niou and Ordeshook point out, "Despite the proliferation of competing models of deterrence, bargaining, coalitions, threats, and so on, those models are rarely set against each other for competitive empirical assessment."[27]

Furthermore, just as a chain of weak links will not bear much weight, a stream of models whose individual insights are familiar or unsurprising will not make much of a contribution. Zagare complains that I focused on only one of his many articles and suggests that the corpus of his recent work does yield more powerful new insights. If one looks at his other works, however, important new insights are hard to discern. He claims that it is a major advance to construct a theory of deterrence in which "threat credibility is a variable," but

---

24. See Robert Jervis, "Cooperation under the Security Dilemma," *World Politics,* Vol. 30, No. 2 (January 1978), pp. 167–214; and Robert Powell, "Absolute and Relative Gains in International Relations Theory," *American Political Science Review,* Vol. 85, No. 4 (December 1991), pp. 1303–1320.
25. Martin, "The Contributions of Rational Choice," pp. 74, 76.
26. On this general point, see Donald N. McCloskey, *Knowledge and Persuasion in Economics,* (Chicago: University of Chicago Press, 1994), chaps. 10, 13.
27. See Niou and Ordeshook, "Return of the Luddites," p. 84.

the variable nature of threat credibility has been recognized as a central element of the theory since the 1960s.[28] Similarly, in "Assessing Competing Defense Postures," Zagare and Kilgour find that "a deterrence equilibrium . . . can occur under almost any conditions, provided that the players have an existential fear of escalation." Turning briefly to the real world, they explain the absence of war between the United States and the Soviet Union by arguing that "the Soviet Union, while motivated to expand, was unwilling to fight a costly strategic war to do so and U.S. leaders knew it." They admit that they cannot explain why limited wars did occur at various points in the Cold War (in their words, such conflicts "lie outside the parameters of the present model"), and they conclude by agreeing with Jervis that "a rational strategy for the employment of nuclear weapons is a contradiction in terms."[29] Readers with a particular interest in the minutiae of abstract bargaining theory may find these arguments creative and original, but scholars who are interested in the real world are unlikely to find their understanding enhanced by reading these works.

In sum, developing a formal theory can be a creative act, and formal theorists do offer new ideas on occasion. On the whole, however, the production of new ideas and hypotheses is not impressive. Among other things, much of the recent formal work suffers from the diminishing returns common to "normal science." Once an initial theoretical breakthrough is made, formalization is one way to refine, qualify, or extend the results. As I have said repeatedly, these contributions can be useful. But the added value generally declines as scholars pursue increasingly rarified results. I therefore stand by my original statement that "formal theory enjoys no particular advantage as a source of theoretical creativity" (p. 30). And although I share Powell's belief that the best way to judge a body of scholarship is to read it one's self, most readers who take the time to do so will reach the same conclusion that I did.

---

28. See Zagare, "All Mortis, No Rigor," p. 112; and Thomas C. Schelling, *Arms and Influence* (New Haven, Conn.: Yale University Press, 1966), especially chap. 2.
29. See Frank C. Zagare and D. Marc Kilgour, "Assessing Competing Defense Postures: The Strategic Implications of Flexible Response," *World Politics*, Vol. 47, No. 3 (April 1995), pp. 400, 403–404, 406–407. In another article, Zagare and Kilgour discover that "the strategic position of a defender without a credible first-stage threat is not enviable," which was precisely the critique of massive retaliation offered by critics like William W. Kaufmann in the 1950s. They also find that "if credibility is considered to vary only across issues, the model suggests that confrontations are least likely as the issues becomes less salient to one side or the other." And when considering why nuclear war did not occur in the 1950s (when U.S. strategy was allegedly one of "massive retaliation"), they admit that "the model provides no obvious answer to this question." See Zagare and Kilgour, "Modeling Massive Retaliation," *Conflict Management and Peace Science*, Vol. 13, No. 1 (Fall 1993), pp. 78–79.

Testing 1, 2, 3 . . .

In "Rigor or Rigor Mortis?" I argued that formal modelers have placed relatively little weight on empirical testing. Many formal articles offer no empirical
evaluation at all, and some of the more ambitious efforts to provide empirical
tests do not achieve a high standard of scholarly rigor. My critics do not offer
a serious challenge to this assessment.

First, neither Bueno de Mesquita and Morrow nor Niou and Ordeshook
devote much effort to defending the empirical validity of the works I criticized
in my article, and the defenses they do offer are not convincing. Bueno de
Mesquita does not even try to defend the case studies in *War and Reason* and
now says that they were merely intended "to illustrate the intuition behind the
model's logic and not as evidence."[30] He defends the quantitative evidence in
the book by citing two recent articles (one of them a revised version of a paper
cited by me, the other a forthcoming article). If one actually reads these articles,
however, it is difficult to see how he can regard them as supporting the claims
made in his book. According to one of the authors he cites, "All we can say
about the [Bueno de Mesquita and Lalman] model is that the percentage of
cases correctly predicted (CP) is between 1% and 41%. As a reference, a null
model that always predicted Status Quo would correctly predict 34% of the
observations. So, *if we were to give the international interaction game the greatest
benefit of doubt possible,* it would predict 21% better than the modal category."
This same author concludes that "there is less support for the international
interaction game than Bueno de Mesquita and Lalman claim."[31] With "support" like this, who needs criticism?

Niou and Ordeshook, by contrast, appear to back away from the idea of
rigorous testing at all. Instead of defending the empirical evidence provided
in their book, they counter by declaring that "reality is far too complicated to
be accommodated in any straightforward way by any simple tractable model,"
and that "scientific testing is an imprecise, often informal process." This reasoning is used to justify their heavy reliance on ad hoc arguments in the
empirical portions of their book: "To suppose that a formal model can wholly

---

30. Bueno de Mesquita and Morrow, "Sorting Through the Wealth of Notions," p. 68.
31. See Curtis S. Signorino, "Strategic Interaction and the Statistical Analysis of International
Conflict," *American Political Science Review,* Vol. 93, No. 2 (June 1999), pp. 290, 292, 294 (emphasis
added). A second paper cited by Bueno de Mesquita and Morrow concludes that "although the
data suggest that Bueno de Mesquita's composite measures influence decision making during
crises, the results are still weak." See Alastair Smith, "Testing Theories of Strategic Choice: The
Example of Crisis Escalation," paper presented at the annual meeting of the American Political
Science Association," Boston, Massachusetts, September 3–6, 1998, p. 21.

encompass a complex process . . . without resorting to some ad hoc discussion is ludicrous."[32] I agree that all theories simplify reality and that testing can be an imprecise business, but it is hard to be impressed when a model employs assumptions that are wildly at odds with our empirical knowledge and when the fit between theory and evidence *depends* on ad hoc factors that contradict the main elements of the theory. Among other things, the model presented in *The Balance of Power* assumes that war is costless, that a state's entire stock of resources can be transferred costlessly to another state, and that all states have complete information about one another's strength. Given these unrealistic assumptions, it is perhaps not surprising that "the notion of 'ceding' [territory], which is central to the model, is virtually absent from the history" to which it is applied.[33] Their model is not an unavoidable simplification of an admittedly complex reality; it is an artificial creation that bears little resemblance to the empirical world they are attempting to analyze.

Second, several of my critics suggest that I employ a double standard on this issue, noting that I praised nonformal theorists like Kenneth Waltz and Robert Jervis despite the lack of empirical testing in their work.[34] In fact, although I admire the work of Waltz, Jervis, Schelling, and others, I believe their work would be better had they devoted greater effort to testing their claims empirically. Some of Schelling's ideas about coercion do not work very well when they are brought into the real world, and those of us who have tried to test Waltz's neorealist balance-of-power theory have found it necessary to modify the theory in order to conform to historical experience.[35] Thus there is no double standard at work here.

Third, several of my critics suggest that modelers do not need to test their conjectures themselves, because there can be a division of labor between scholars who derive hypotheses and those who test them.[36] I agree that individual scholars have different comparative advantages and that expecting

32. Niou and Ordeshook, "Return of the Luddites," pp. 93–94.
33. See Emerson M.S. Niou, Peter C. Ordeshook, and Gregory F. Rose, *The Balance of Power: Stability in International Systems* (Cambridge: Cambridge University Press, 1989); and Glenn Snyder, "Alliances, Balance, and Stability," *International Organization*, Vol. 45, No. 1 (Winter 1991), p. 137.
34. See Powell, "The Modeling Enterprise and Security Studies," p. 104; and Niou and Ordeshook, "Return of the Luddites," p. 90.
35. On Schelling, see Wallace J. Thies, *When Governments Collide: Coercion and Diplomacy in the Vietnam Conflict, 1964–1968* (Berkeley: University of California Press, 1980); and Robert A. Pape, *Bombing to Win: Air Power and Coercion in War* (Ithaca, N.Y.: Cornell University Press, 1996). On Waltz, see Stephen M. Walt, *The Origins of Alliances* (Ithaca, N.Y.: Cornell University Press, 1987), pp. 21–22, 263–264.
36. See Bueno de Mesquita and Morrow, "Sorting Through the Wealth of Notions," p. 71; and Zagare, "All Mortis, No Rigor," p. 114.

many modelers to do careful empirical testing may not be an efficient allocation of their talents. My point, however, was that the modeling community as a whole has tended to place a low value on this criterion. More important, the argument that the scholarly community can rely upon a division of labor is convincing only if one is committed to maintaining a diverse array of scholars in the field. As discussed below, however, it is not clear that this is what most formal modelers seek.

Policy Relevance

Several respondents argue that formal models have made a significant contribution to real-world policy debates. I do not deny that formal modelers have written on policy-relevant topics in a few cases, but as I said in my article, they "have joined in only after the central parameters were established by others" (p. 47). I stand by my original assertion, therefore, and most of my critics do not challenge it. Moreover, I see little evidence that the policy community has paid much attention to recent formal work, or that policymakers would gain much real-world insight if they did. For example, has the vast formal literature on crisis bargaining produced insights or lessons that might actually help someone who was trying to manage a real-world crisis? What novel and practical lessons have been derived from the abstract discussions of nuclear deterrence found in the writings of prominent formal theorists? By contrast, more concrete explorations of deterrence policy by scholars such as Bruce Blair, John Steinbruner, and Scott Sagan have identified important dangers, suggested a variety of useful remedies, and attracted considerable attention in both the academic and policy worlds.[37]

The boldest challenge to my claims about the irrelevance of much of the recent formal work comes from Bueno de Mesquita and Morrow, who argue that Bueno de Mesquita's applied forecasting model is "a practical tool for policy analysis." They quote testimony from a government official suggesting that the model has an accuracy rate of 90 percent and declare that "the United States government . . . finds the model accurate and . . . uses the model to assist with important foreign policy matters."[38]

---

37. See Bruce G. Blair, *Strategic Command and Control: Redefining the Nuclear Threat* (Washington, D.C.: Brookings, 1985); John D. Steinbruner, "Beyond Rational Deterrence: The Struggle for New Conceptions," *World Politics*, Vol. 28, No. 2 (January 1976), pp. 223–242; and Scott D. Sagan, *The Limits of Safety: Organizations, Accidents, and Nuclear Weapons* (Princeton, N.J.: Princeton University Press, 1993).

38. See Bueno de Mesquita and Morrow, "Sorting Through the Wealth of Notions," p. 70.

Space does not permit a detailed critique of these claims, but such assertions should be taken with many grains of salt. First, although Bueno de Mesquita has described his model in general terms, the published descriptions of the forecasting model are not sufficiently detailed to permit others to replicate all of his results. Such opacity makes sense from a commercial point of view, but in science, transparency should take precedence over preserving market share.

Second, Bueno de Mesquita's claims to predictive accuracy are questionable. Without access to the full range of predictions made by the model, it is impossible to tell just how accurate it is or how many novel predictions it actually makes. But the published record of the forecasting model is not impressive. One article "predicts" the U.S. victory in the Cold War; unfortunately, the article was written six years after the Soviet Union collapsed.[39] Another article attempts to forecast the Middle East peace negotiations, but fails to anticipate either the mechanism by which the process occurred or the final outcome.[40] Similarly, a coauthored book forecasting the fate of Hong Kong offers a host of familiar generalities (for which no model was needed), along with a number of more specific and controversial predictions that have not fared well thus far.[41]

---

39. See Bruce Bueno de Mesquita, "The End of the Cold War: Predicting an Emergent Property," *Journal of Conflict Resolution*, Vol. 42, No. 2 (April 1998), pp. 131–155. Bueno de Mesquita performs 100 simulations using the model and discovers that the United States wins the Cold War in the majority of them. This result is not surprising, insofar as the United States began the Cold War with three times the gross national product of the Soviet Union and a superior geopolitical position. For a more prescient prediction, consider Kenneth N. Waltz's 1979 forecast that "with half of our GNP [gross national product], [the Soviet Union] nevertheless has to run hard to stay in the race. One may think that question is not whether a third or fourth country will enter the circle of great powers . . . but rather whether the Soviet Union can keep up." Similarly, my own analysis of the Cold War (published in 1987) argued that "the most important causes of security cooperation among states combine to favor [the United States]. . . . The principal causes of alliance formation work to its advantage and isolate the Soviet Union from virtually all of the world's strategically significant states." See Waltz, *Theory of International Politics* (Reading, Mass.: Addison-Wesley, 1979), pp. 179–180; and Walt, *Origins of Alliances*, chap. 8, especially pp. 284–285.
40. See Bruce Bueno de Mesquita, "Multilateral Negotiations: A Spatial Analysis of the Arab-Israeli Dispute," *International Organization*, Vol. 44, No. 3 (Summer 1990), pp. 317–340. Among other things, the model assumes that the Soviet Union is as powerful a player as the United States in 1990 and fails to anticipate the Soviet collapse in 1991. The model predicts that Israeli-Palestinian negotiations would yield "nothing approaching even a semiautonomous state," and that "there appears to be no reason to anticipate more than modest concessions by the Israelis to the interests of the Palestinians in the near future." Ibid., pp. 337, 340. In fact, Israel did make important concessions during the peace process, and the Palestinians are very close to having their own state.
41. For example, the authors claim that "the succession [to Deng Xiaoping] will be clouded by severe infighting" featuring "several rounds of brutal exchanges," and suggest that "the [Communist] party will hold on to some power and perhaps nobody will win." The prediction is not very precise, but signs of severe infighting have been notably absent thus far. They also predict that "there is likely to be a sudden and dramatic collapse of support for market reforms" within a year

Lastly, the evidence that the "U.S. government . . . uses the model to assist on important foreign policy matters" is dubious. Bueno de Mesquita's claims rest on the testimony of one midlevel Central Intelligence Agency official and an *Izvestiya* article recounting a briefing by unnamed U.S. "officials." One midlevel bureaucrat does not equal the "U.S. government," however, and two former directors of the National Intelligence Council (which prepares National Intelligence Estimates) and a former deputy director for intelligence have reported that they were not aware that Bueno de Mesquita's model had any impact on the estimation process or on policy. According to one of these officials, models like Bueno de Mesquita's are primarily useful "to stimulate questions for further research and study."[42] Based on the evidence to date, this forecasting model is a weak reed upon which to base a claim to real-world relevance.

Methodological Pluralism

A central theme of my article was the importance of methodological diversity. Specifically, I pointed out that security studies has always been "theoretically and methodologically diverse," and "the field as a whole will be richer if such diversity is retained *and esteemed*" (pp. 8, 47–48, emphasis in original).

Given my position, Martin's data showing that formal modelers do not "dominate" the field is beside the point. The issue is not whether a particular group or methodological technique is currently hegemonic; it is whether any group has hegemonic *ambitions.* After all, the time to resist hegemony is before an imperialist movement becomes too strong to resist, not after it has established itself in a position of predominance.

Let us be candid. There is a widespread perception that formal modelers are less tolerant of other approaches than virtually any other group in the field of

---

or two of the Chinese takeover of Hong Kong, and forecast "that Hong Kong's autonomy will be eroded quickly, only to be restored for a period of a year or so." Neither development has occurred. They predict a dramatic decline in press freedom in Hong Kong (which has not transpired), and suggest that an important bellwether would be the suppression of demonstrations in Hong Kong commemorating the Tiananmen Square uprising on June 4, 1989. So far, demonstrations have been permitted. They correctly predict an economic slowdown in Hong Kong and in China itself, but this decline was the result of the East Asian financial crisis rather than the transition to communist rule. Nor has the value of the Hong Kong dollar declined significantly, despite the pressures created by the financial crisis. For their original forecasts, see Bruce Bueno de Mesquita, David Newman, and Alvin Rabushka, *Red Flag over Hong Kong?* (Chatham, N.J.: Chatham House, 1996), pp. 8–9, 94, 97–98, 126–127, 129–130.

42. Personal correspondence with Joseph Nye, Richard Cooper, and Douglas McEachin.

political science. This is not true of every scholar who uses formal methods, but it is striking how widespread the belief is and equally striking to note that formal modelers are the only group in our profession that is regarded in this way.

Do my critics' responses lend support to these concerns? Sadly, yes. Although several of them pay lip service to the principle of methodological pluralism, their disregard for nonformal approaches is apparent. As noted above, Niou and Ordeshook clearly regard most scholarship in political science as primitive at best, and they deride those who find formal work needlessly obscure as Luddites "who studied French and Plato in college rather than calculus." (For the record, I studied all three). Niou and Ordeshook's contempt is even more apparent when they write that there is nothing in the field of strategic studies that deserves the label of "theory," or when they refer to the scholarly study of real-world problems as "mere journalism, until it can be given the solid scientific grounding that formal theorists pursue."[43] Similarly, although Bueno de Mesquita and Morrow endorse my claim that "security studies should welcome contributions from formal theory," their failure to include the rest of the sentence (which calls for the inclusion of "large-N statistical analysis, historical case studies, and even the more rigorous forms of interpretive or constructivist analysis," p. 48) is revealing. The question is: Do they share my belief that each of these methods should be "retained *and esteemed?"* Finally, Martin's claim that "as scientific fields . . . develop, they invariably become more mathematical" betrays a belief that over time, nonformal approaches should be relegated to the dustbin of history (or history departments).[44] Some branches of science have become highly mathematical, but others (such as biology and geology) retain a large and important qualitative dimension. In any event, the record to date does not suggest that formal models in security studies are superior to other research traditions.

Finally, we should not forget that a professed commitment to pluralism is "cheap talk." It is easy to say one is in favor of other approaches, but the real question is how different scholars react when allocating scarce resources. This is an empirical question, and all members of the field are free to participate in the research project. Over time, we can all keep track of which methodological subfields show signs of imperialist tendencies, consistently favoring their own

43. Niou and Ordeshook, "Return of the Luddites, pp. 87, 93, 96.
44. Martin, "Contributions of Rational Choice," p. 78.

tribe over others.[45] Needless to say, concerns about the imperialistic tendencies of formal modelers will decline if they are willing to endorse and support scholars whose work uses other well-established techniques, rather than exhibiting a clear and consistent preference for other formal modelers.

Conclusion

Scholarship is a competitive enterprise, and knowledge advances partly through the clashes of competing ideas. Yet the competition that drives progress should be tempered with the recognition that different research traditions can and should coexist. Just as biodiversity is central to a healthy ecosystem, intellectual diversity is an important part of a healthy scholarly community. In the past, security studies has profited by welcoming contributions from a diverse array of historians, political scientists, economists, natural scientists, psychologists, and others. The field has been methodologically and theoretically wide-ranging, but united by a close concern with real-world policy issues. This combination of diversity has enabled scholars with different backgrounds and talents to profit from one another's contributions, thereby allowing the field as a whole to advance more swiftly than it would were any single tradition to extinguish the others.

In short, there are good reasons to encourage a diversity of research approaches within any subfield as important as security studies. Because there is scientific value in each of the established traditions of contemporary social science research, the field of security studies will be impoverished if any single approach becomes hegemonic.

---

45. Lest I again be accused of a double standard, I offer the following data. During my ten years as a tenured faculty member at the University of Chicago, there were eleven occasions where my department voted to hire, renew, or promote a formal modeler. I voted in favor nine times and voted to oppose twice, a percentage similar to my record on nonformal candidates.

Suggestions for Further Reading

There is a huge and expanding literature on rational choice approaches and formal models. This list is not meant to be exhaustive, but it includes many works relevant to the themes of this volume.

Rational Choice and Formal Methods: General and Introductory Works

These works offer descriptions of rational choice theory and many are textbooks on the mathematical tools used in formal models. Several also discuss the potential benefits of these approaches.

Alt, James, and Kenneth Shepsle, eds. *Perspectives on Positive Political Economy.* Cambridge, U.K.: Cambridge University Press, 1990.

Elster, Jon, ed. *Rational Choice.* New York: New York University Press, 1986.

Lalman, David, Joe Oppenheimer, and Piotr Swistak. "Formal Rational Choice Theory: A Cumulative Science of Politics." In Ada W. Finifter, ed., *Political Science: State of the Discipline II.* Washington, D.C.: American Political Science Association, 1993, pp. pp. 77–104.

Morrow, James D. *Game Theory for Political Scientists.* Princeton, N.J.: Princeton University Press, 1994.

Mueller, Dennis, ed. *Public Choice II.* Cambridge, U.K.: Cambridge University Press, 1989.

Ordeshook, Peter C. *Game Theory and Political Theory: An Introduction.* Cambridge, U.K.: Cambridge University Press, 1986.

Ordeshook, Peter C., ed. *Models of Strategic Choice in Politics.* Ann Arbor: University of Michigan Press, 1989.

Shepsle, Kenneth A., and Mark S. Bonchek. *Analyzing Politics.* New York: Norton, 1997.

Classic Explications and Applications of Rational Choice Approaches

These works include the pioneering elaborations of how game theory and other rational choice approaches could be applied to social, economic, and political problems. Von Neumann and Morgenstern is the *locus classicus.* Other works listed here apply the insights of rational choice theory, often without the use of formal models.

Arrow, Kenneth. *Social Choice and Individual Values.* New York: Wiley, 1951.

Downs, Anthony. *An Economic Theory of Democracy.* New York: Harper and Row, 1957.

Luce, R. Duncan, and Howard Raiffa. *Games and Decisions: Introduction and Critical Survey.* New York: Wiley, 1957.

Olson, Mancur. *The Logic of Collective Action: Public Goods and the Theory of Groups.* Cambridge, Mass.: Harvard University Press, 1965.

Rapaport, Anatol. *Fights, Games, and Debates.* Ann Arbor: University of Michigan Press, 1960.

Riker, William H. *The Theory of Political Coalitions.* New Haven, Conn.: Yale University Press, 1962.

Schelling, Thomas C. *Choice and Consequence.* Cambridge, Mass.: Harvard University Press, 1984.

Schelling, Thomas C. *The Strategy of Conflict.* Cambridge, Mass.: Harvard University Press, 1960.

Simon, Herbert. *Models of Man: Social and Rational.* New York: Wiley, 1957.

Tullock, Gordon, and James Buchanan, eds. *The Calculus of Consent.* Ann Arbor: University of Michigan Press, 1962.

Von Neumann, John, and Oskar Morgenstern. *Theory of Games and Economic Behavior.* Princeton, N.J.: Princeton University Press, 1944.

Critiques, Assessments, and Defenses of Rational Choice Approaches

The following works offer criticism and support for rational choice approaches, sometimes in the same volume. The best-known comprehensive critique of rational choice in political science is Page and Shapiro, *Pathologies of Rational Choice*. Rebuttals to Page and Shaprio, and their response, appear in Friedman, ed., *The Rational Choice Controversy*. Robert Bates and Chalmers Johnson engage in a spirited debate over the role of rational choice theory in area studies.

Bates, Robert. "Area Studies and the Discipline: A Useful Controversy." *PS: Political Science and Politics*, Vol. 30, No. 2 (June 1997), pp. 166–169.

Friedman, Jeffrey, ed. *The Rational Choice Controversy: Economic Models of Politics Reconsidered.* New Haven, Conn: Yale University Press, 1996.

Green, Donald, and Ian Shapiro. *Pathologies of Rational Choice Theory: A Critique of Applications in Political Science.* New Haven, Conn.: Yale University Press, 1995.

Grofman, Bernard. "On The Gentle Art of Rational Choice Bashing." In Bernard Grofman, ed. *Information, Participation, and Choice: An Economic Theory of Democracy in Perspective.* Ann Arbor: University of Michigan Press, 1993, pp. 239–242.

Jervis, Robert. "Models and Cases in the Study of International Conflict." *Journal of International Affairs*, Vol. 44, No. 1 (Spring/Summer 1990), pp. 81–102.

Johnson, Chalmers, and E.B. Keehn. "A Disaster in the Making: Rational Choice and Asian Studies." *The National Interest*, No. 36 (Summer 1994), pp. 14–22.

Johnson, Chalmers. "Preconception vs. Observation, or the Contributions of Rational Choice Theory and Area Studies to Contemporary Political Science." *PS: Political Science and Politics*, Vol. 30, No. 2 (June 1997), pp. 170–174.

Monroe, Kristen Renwick, ed. *The Economic Approach to Politics: A Critical Assessment of the Theory of Rational Choice.* New York: HarperCollins, 1991.

"Rational Choice Theory and Politics." Special issue of *Critical Review*, Vol. 9, Nos. 1–2 (Winter-Spring 1995).

Rule, James B. *Theory and Progress in Social Science*. Cambridge, U.K.: Cambridge University Press, 1997, chap. 3.

Udehn, Lars. *The Limits of Public Choice: A Sociological Critique of the Economic Theory of Politics*. New York: Routledge, 1996.

Wolfinger, Raymond. "The Rational Citizen Faces Election Day, or What Rational Choice Theories Don't Tell You about American Elections." In M. Kent Jennings and Thomas E. Mann, eds., *Elections at Home and Abroad: Essays in Honor of Warren E. Miller*. Ann Arbor: University of Michigan Press, 1993.

Rational Choice and International Security Studies

The works listed here are only a small portion of the burgeoning security studies literature that uses formal models and rational choice approaches. In selecting these works, we have attempted to include the books and articles frequently cited and discussed in this volume. We also have leaned toward including books and articles from journals that are readily accessible.

Banks, Jeffrey S. "Equilibrium Behavior in Crisis Bargaining Games." *American Journal of Political Science*, Vol. 34, No. 3 (August 1990), pp. 599–614.

Brams, Steven J. *Superpower Games: Applying Game Theory to Superpower Conflict*. New Haven, Conn.: Yale University Press, 1985.

Brams, Steven J., and D. Marc Kilgour. *Game Theory and National Security*. New York: Blackwell, 1988.

Bueno de Mesquita, Bruce. *The War Trap*. New Haven, Conn.: Yale University Press, 1981.

Bueno de Mesquita, Bruce, and David Lalman. *War and Reason: Domestic and International Imperatives*. New Haven, Conn.: Yale University Press, 1992.

Bueno de Mesquita, Bruce, James D. Morrow, Randolph M. Siverson, and Alastair Smith. "An Institutional Explanation of the Democratic Peace." *American Political Science Review*, Vol. 93, No. 4 (December 1999), pp. 791–807.

Downs, George, and David Rocke. *Optimal Imperfection?* Princeton, N.J.: Princeton University Press, 1995.

Downs, George, and David Rocke. *Tacit Bargaining and Arms Control*. Ann Arbor: University of Michigan Press, 1989.

Fearon, James D. "Domestic Audience Costs and the Escalation of International Disputes." *American Political Science Review*, Vol. 88, No. 3 (September 1994), pp. 577–592.

Fearon, James D. "Rationalist Explanations of War." *International Organization*, Vol. 49, No. 3 (Summer 1995), pp. 379–414.

Fearon, James D. "Signaling Versus the Balance of Power and Interests." *Journal of Conflict Resolution*, Vol. 38, No. 2 (June 1994), pp. 236–269.

Fearon, James D. and David Laitin. "Explaining Interethnic Cooperation." *American Political Science Review*, Vol. 90, No. 4 (December 1996), pp. 715–735.

Kilgour, D. Marc, and Frank C. Zagare. "Credibility, Uncertainty, and Deterrence." *American Journal of Political Science*, Vol. 35, No. 2 (May 1991), pp. 305–334.

Kim, Woosang, and James D. Morrow. "When Do Power Shifts Lead to War?" *American Journal of Political Science*, Vol. 36, No. 4 (November 1992), pp. 896–922.

Kydd, Andrew. "Game Theory and the Spiral Model." *World Politics*, Vol. 49, No. 3 (April 1997), pp. 371–400.

Lake, David A. and Robert Powell, eds. *Strategic Choice and International Relations.* Princeton, N.J.: Princeton University Press, 1999.

Lalman, David, and David Newman. "Alliance Formation and National Security." *International Interactions*, Vol. 16, No. 4 (1991), pp. 239–254.

Levy, Jack S. "Prospect Theory, Rational Choice, and International Relations." *International Studies Quarterly*, Vol. 41, No. 1 (March 1997), pp. 87–112.

Morrow, James D. " Alliances, Credibility, and Peacetime Costs." *Journal of Conflict Resolution*, Vol. 38, No. 2 (June 1994), pp. 270–297.

Morrow, James D. "Capabilities, Uncertainty, and Resolve: A Limited Information Model of Crisis Bargaining." *American Journal of Political Science*, Vol. 33, No. 4 (November 1989), pp. 941–972.

Morrow, James D. "Electoral and Congressional Incentives and Arms Control." *Journal of Conflict Resolution*, Vol. 35, No. 2 (June 1991), pp. 243–263.

Morrow, James D. "When Do 'Relative Gains' Impede Trade?" *Journal of Conflict Resolution*, Vol. 41, No. 1 (February 1997), pp. 12–37.

Nalebuff, Barry. "Rational Deterrence in an Imperfect World." *World Politics*, Vol. 43, No. 3 (April 1991), pp. 313–335.

Nicholson, Michael. *Rationality and the Analysis of International Conflict.* Cambridge, U.K.: Cambridge University Press, 1992.

Niou, Emerson M.S., Peter Ordeshook, and Gregory F. Rose. *The Balance of Power: Stability in International Systems.* Cambridge, U.K.: Cambridge University Press, 1989.

Olson, Mancur, and Richard Zeckhauser. "An Economic Theory of Alliances." *Review of Economics and Statistics*, Vol. 48, No. 3 (August 1966), pp. 266–279.

O'Neill, Barry. "Game Theory and the Study of Deterrence in War." In Paul C. Stern, Robert Axelrod, Robert Jervis, and Roy Radner, eds., *Perspectives on Deterrence.* New York: Oxford University Press, 1989), pp. 134–156.

O'Neill, Barry. "Game Theory Models of Peace and War." In Robert Aumann and Sergiu Hart, eds., *Handbook of Game Theory with Economic Applications*, Vol. 2. Amsterdam: Elsevier Science, 1994, chapter 29.

Powell, Robert. "Absolute and Relative Gains in International Relations Theory." *American Political Science Review*, Vol. 85, No. 4 (December 1991), pp. 1303–1320.

Powell, Robert. *In the Shadow of Power.* Princeton, N.J.: Princeton University Press, 1999.

Powell, Robert. *Nuclear Deterrence Theory: The Search for Credibility.* Cambridge, U.K.: Cambridge University Press, 1990.

Schultz, Kenneth A. "Do Democratic Institutions Constrain or Inform?" *International Organization*, Vol. 53, No. 2 (Spring 1999), pp. 233–266.

Schultz, Kenneth A. "Domestic Opposition and Signaling in International Crises." *American Political Science Review*, Vol . 92, No. 4 (December 1998), pp. 829–844.

Signorino, Curtis S. "Strategic Interaction and the Statistical Analysis of International Conflict." *American Political Science Review*, Vol. 93, No. 2 (June 1999), pp. 279–297.

Smith, Alastair. "Alliance Formation and War." *International Studies Quarterly*, Vol. 39, No. 4 (December 1995), pp. 405–425.

Snidal, Duncan. "The Game *Theory* of International Politics." *World Politics*, Vol. 38, No. 1 (October 1985), pp. 25–57.

Verba, Sidney. "Assumptions of Rationality and Non-Rationality in Models of the International System." *World Politics*, Vol. 14, No. 1 (October 1961), pp. 93–117.

Wagner, R. Harrison. "The Theory of Games and the Problem of International Cooperation." *American Political Science Review*, Vol. 77, No. 2 (June 1983), pp. 330–346.

Wagner, R. Harrison. "War and Expected-Utility Theory." [A review article on Bueno de Mesquita, *The War Trap*.] *World Politics*, Vol. 36, No. 3 (April 1984), pp. 407–423.

Zagare, "Rationality and Deterrence." *World Politics*, Vol. 42, No. 2 (January 1990), pp. 238–260.

Zagare, Frank C., and D. Marc Kilgour. *Perfect Deterrence*. New York: Cambridge University Press, forthcoming 1999.

International Security

The Robert and Renée Belfer Center for
Science and International Affairs
John F. Kennedy School of Government
Harvard University

Articles in this reader were previously published in **International Security**, a quarterly journal sponsored and edited by The Robert and Renée Belfer Center for Science and International Affairs at the John F. Kennedy School of Government at Harvard University, and published by MIT Press Journals. To receive subscription information about the journal or find out more about other readers in our series, please contact MIT Press Journals at Five Cambridge Center, Fourth Floor, Cambridge, MA, 02142-1493.